LOVE THAT WOULD NOT LET ME GO

JACKIE CALLOWAY

CHRISTIAN LIVING BOOKS, INC.
AN IMPRINT OF PNEUMA LIFE PUBLISHING
LARGO, MD

Christian Living Books, Inc.
An imprint of Pneuma Life Publishing, Inc.
P.O. Box 7584
Largo, MD 20792
301-218-9092
www.christianlivingbooks.com

ISBN 1-56229-016-9
Printed in the United States of America

Scripture quotations marked "The Amplified Bible" or "AMP" are taken from The Amplified Bible, Old Testament copyright © 1965, 1987 by the Zondervan Corporation and The Amplified New Testament copyright © 1958, 1987 by The Lockman Foundation. Used by permission. All rights reserved.

Unless otherwise marked, all Scripture quotations are taken from the King James Version of the Bible.

In my personal opinion, good writing is not only how you choose to say what you say, but WHAT you choose to say. I thought you did an excellent job of choosing the content. Your ability to express how you felt and how things made you feel is very impressive. The way the book was structured was excellent. Your writing style made for a very interesting book. The little asides you took were great...just enough...not to much. You added just enough spice to make the book more palatable...while remaining tasteful. The book was heart-wrenching where it needed to be, heart-warming where it needed to be, hearty where it needed to be, and heartfelt where it needed to be. Your story had so many levels, it is sure to minister to a wide variety of people. In the end, no matter what kind of trouble the reader may have, the answer is "Love does not let you go." Well done!

—Kimberly Stewart
President
Christian Living Books, Inc.

DEDICATION

dedicate this book to my husband and God's man, Ronnie Calloway, and our beautiful daughters, Margo Smith, Rhonda Williams and Chaunci Clough.

Ronnie, I am overwhelmed when I think of how deeply and tenderly you have loved and supported me for the past ten years. You are the one who told me, constantly, what a great writer I was. You are the one who gave me the freedom and trust to write whatever I felt necessary in this book. You are the one who has yet to read one page of the book, and yet have financed me all the way. I'll thank God for you until my dying day and pray that this book will allow people to see what a mighty man of God you are.

Margo, Rhonda, and Chaunci, I dedicate this book to you because all three of you have been the sunshine of my life. I want to convey to you, through the completion of this book, that you can do and be all that God is calling you to be. I want you to remember that through Christ ALL things are possible. I have always loved you girls with all that I am. I'm thankful to God for everyday that you have inspired me to live this abundant life because I have you. I pray that I have inspired you–as Mama inspired me–to give my grandchildren Jesus Christ. He will never leave them or forsake them, but will walk them through their lives in victory.

CONTENTS

ACKNOWLEDGMENTS

I must first and foremost acknowledge God the Father, God the Son and God the Holy Spirit, Who told me to write this book and directed my paths in doing so.

Debbie Kirton, who showed me how to get started and pushed me to just keep writing.

Deborah Chase, who helped me with the computer whenever I got stuck.

Lauren Wilhoite-Willis, who for more than a year, edited the content and copy tirelessly. You encouraged me in more ways than I can express. (You would not have this book in your hands today had it not been for her friendship, expertise and dedication to the completion of this project.)

I also must acknowledge Bishop Rayfield and Rita Whittington, my pastors, who continually push and encourage me to fulfill my God-given purpose, and to get out of me all God has put in me.

PROLOGUE

The morning dawned. As I open my eyes, immediately my heart pounds within me like a big bass drum. I have the stark realization that this is The Day, April 19, 1996; this is actually the day.

I lay there motionless as several thoughts try to crowd my mind at once: "What in the world are you doing? Are you sure you want to go through with this? How do you know he has really changed? What if he hurts you again? You've been doing just fine on your own. How did all of this happen anyway? Almost everybody says you're crazy. Are you crazy?"

"Stop, Stop, Stop. I have to stop thinking these thoughts. Get a hold of yourself Jackie, get a grip!" *This is the day the Lord has made and I will rejoice and be glad in it.*

"But I wonder if he's thinking the same thing? I wonder if he's having second thoughts about marrying me. I wonder if he's doing this to pay me back–to hurt me again."

1

"Oh God, have mercy on me," I cry as I clutch my head. It seems as if the devil is sitting on my chest, hurling negative thoughts at my head–one after another...after another. But, *I cast down all these imaginations and every high thing that would exalt itself against the knowledge of God. And I bring every thought into captivity of Jesus Christ.* "God I know you told me to listen to Ronnie; I **know** You did."

Again, I lay motionless. I began to pray, "Dear God, I come to you this morning in the name of Jesus. Lord, *I present my body a living sacrifice, holy and acceptable unto You which is my reasonable service. I'll be not conformed to this world, but I'll be transformed by the renewing of my mind. And Lord, I'll not think more highly of myself than I ought to think, but I will think,* only those thoughts you would have me to think. Lord, *this is the day that You have made, I will rejoice and be glad in it.* Lord, if I'm not supposed to marry Ronnie Calloway tonight, You show me. Even if it's at the altar Lord, You show me and I'll turn around. Father, my only desire is to do Your will."

"Lord, it's remarkable that this is happening. I never dreamed in a million years that I would be in this place today. Father You are Somebody. *You are great and You do wondrous things.* You are God all by Yourself. Lord, I know it was just the devil throwing that doubt at me when I first woke up. *I'm not ignorant of his devices.* Lord, I know You ordained this day before the foundation of the world. I surrender my will to You. Thank You, Father, for being in relentless pursuit of both of us–though we tried to go in different directions. But, today I lay here face to face with the Love, Your *Love that would not let me go.* I pray, in Jesus' name. Thank You Father, Amen."

"Oh, I have so much to do today, let me get up."

It's amazing what happens to me when I pray. Prayer is like removing a big medicine ball that has been lying on my chest for days. I take that ball and with all my might, I toss it to Him. What a relief! All of the pressure is off of me and on to someone who wants it, and can handle it. Whew!

As I brush my teeth, I look into the mirror. "Jackie Calloway, today is your wedding day girl. Whatcha think about that?" I'm just in awe at what God can do when we cooperate with Him. He is allowing me to

marry the very best. The man **He** wants me to marry. To me, Ronnie is the most wonderful, God fearing, loving, gentle, kind, tenderhearted, handsome man on this earth. A man who loves God more than he loves me—which causes him to love me as Christ loves the church.

"Jackie, your eyes are so bright this morning full of wonder and expectation. These eyes are so unlike the eyes you've seen in the mirror in the past. Those eyes were sad, and sometimes full of hurt and tears. But this is a new day, girl! There'll be no more tears and sorrow. Well, not today anyway. Jackie, you actually look happy and joyful. There is a glow that radiates from your cheeks."

Oh, my heart is pounding again like that big bass drum, but this time it's with excitement. I am so happy.

"Now, I have to get all of my things together and go to the Marriott Hotel, where we will spend our wedding night. Tomorrow, we will fly to San Diego for our honeymoon. Can you stand it? Be still my heart. This is so much fun.

"Okay, where is my list? Get my stockings, nail polish, shoes, perfume, negligee– yes, the cute, little, sexy, black, see-through, snap-between-the-legs negligee! Ronnie will love it. I can just see his eyes now, as big as cups, and he'll have a grin as wide as a saucer. Can you stand it? We are going to have the time of our lives. Yahoo!

"Oh Lord, forgive me, but it is still hard for me to believe that I am getting married tonight. I am getting married tonight for the second time…to the same man. The same man I was married to for twenty-eight long years before our devastating divorce. The same man that lied to me, was unfaithful to me over and over again, caused us to lose our home, disappointed and betrayed our children and me. How could I be happy about marrying him again after all he took me through?"

CHAPTER 1

THE SPIRIT THAT CHANGES OUR LIVES

I remember vividly our first wedding day, back in 1965. It was a different scene and a different story. I was only nineteen years old; Ronnie was twenty-one. And, we knew absolutely nothing about anything. I was saved; Ronnie wasn't; We had never heard of being *unequally yoked together* (2 Cor. 6:4) . Even though I grew up in the Baptist church, I did not understand the scriptures for myself. I had been preached to but never taught. We were getting married having only known each other for one month. All we knew was we were both grown and on our own and my Mama gave us her blessing.

Ronnie told me he had never met a girl he thought he wanted to spend the rest of his life with. Therefore, he wanted to marry me…as soon as possible. Being the country girl from West Virginia that I was, the attention was flattering and almost irresistible.

$\mathscr{L}$OVE THAT WOULD NOT LET ME GO

Why do I say *almost* irresistible? Because when I was about ten years old, an old woman, Mrs. Washington, told me, "Jackie, if you pray and ask God to send you the husband He has for you, He will send him and you won't get a divorce." So, when Ronnie asked me to marry him, I prayed and asked God if this was that man. He said yes. That's why I said yes to Ronnie so quickly. God did not tell me to marry him. I believe He wanted Ronnie born again first, but that didn't happen.

On our first wedding day, as I was getting dressed, I remember looking out of the window of the church. I saw Ronnie and his best man drinking whiskey from a bottle in a paper bag...in front of the church. I should have known right then that we would have a bumpy road ahead. We did indeed.

YOU'VE BEEN WHIPPED

The first two years were actually very good for me. Ronnie treated me kindly and as though he really did love me. When our daughter, Rhonda, was born, he said, "Now I know what love really is." He did not have a clue what real love was yet. His lifestyle displayed the opposite of true love. There were other women, even then. I was so naïve that I believed everything he told me. There were always unexplained absences. He would say, "I'm going to the store" or "I have to make a run" and would be gone four and five hours at a time. This, mind you, happened almost every day. I'm sure some of those women he was with are reading this book right now.

By the time our youngest daughter, Chaunci, was born in 1969, things were real shaky, to say the least. People came to my house to tell me **who** Ronnie was doing this week. He would stay out all night, come home smelling like perfume, and tell me it was all in my mind. Within a few months, I became very ill from the stress of it all. I went from one hundred and forty pounds to one hundred and six pounds. I am five feet seven inches tall.

During that time, I went home to visit my mother in Huntington, West Virginia. When she saw how thin and stressed I looked she said, "What has happened to you? I wouldn't let a man do me like this."

I said, "Oh Mama, I just worry about things more than I should. At least he's not beating me. I have some girlfriends who are being whipped for breakfast, lunch and dinner."

She said, "Uh, you've been whipped and don't know it." That statement slapped me into reality.

I HAD ANOTHER LOVER

When I got filled with the Holy Spirit in 1974, my life began to change for the better. After that life-changing event, I began to have a revelation of who Jesus is, and who I am in Him.

I never knew anything about being filled with the Holy Spirit. When I was a teenager, I did ask my Baptist pastor about speaking in other tongues. He told me that all of those upper room disciples in the book of Acts were from different countries and they were speaking in their native tongues. Not true. All the disciples were Jewish and from that area. Nonetheless, as they began to speak in other tongues, the people who were outside the upper room heard their native tongues coming from the mouths of these unlearned men.

All I know is when I saw that our lives were going to pot, I knew the only one Who could save us and our marriage was the Lord Jesus Christ. I prayed and asked Him to please help us.

I think it was the next day, Sandra True, an old girlfriend of mine, whom I had not seen for months, came to my house. As we were catching up on each other's lives, she told me I needed to be filled with the Holy Ghost. I told her, with my hand on my hip, "I am filled with the Holy Ghost. The Lord answers my prayers." She asked, "With the evidence of speaking in other tongues?"

"I don't know about any speaking in other tongues," I retorted, "but I know I'm filled with the Holy Ghost." When Sandra left my house, however, I was so desperate that I went into the bathroom and prayed. "Lord, what is this talking in tongues thing? Is that of You? You know Lord, I want all of You that I can get or Ronnie and I are not going to make it."

Well, to my surprise, I came right out of the bathroom to a preacher teaching on the radio about being filled with the Holy Spirit with the evidence of speaking in other tongues. I was absolutely floored. I sat down and listened intently with my Bible in hand. I found out that it is scriptural to talk in other tongues, according to Acts chapter two–and in many other places in the New Testament. I was so excited.

Immediately, I prayed, asking the Lord to fill me with the Holy Spirit…and nothing happened. For weeks, I went to church service after church service trying, to get filled with the Holy Spirit…but nothing happened.

A few weeks passed and my children became very close with Sandra's children. Our children were the same age and played together often. One day, Sandra called and said she was sending my children home and that they had a surprise for me. When I saw them coming down the street, I could see there was something different about them. They seemed to be glowing. When they got to me they said, "Mom, we got filled with the Holy Ghost." They began to speak in other tongues. They were six and nine years old.

Again, I was floored. But this time I was upset. "Why can't I get filled with the Spirit? What's wrong with me?" Of course I thought of everything. I'm not good enough; there is still sin in my life; maybe I need to tarry." I wanted to be filled with the Spirit so badly that I told the Lord, "If you don't fill me with Your Spirit, I don't want to live." I've learned that sometimes we can say some stupid things in desperation. I'm sure our Father says, "I know she didn't go there did she?" But I really meant that. I was so hungry for all of what God had for me that I knew I couldn't have peace until it happened.

But then…I was in my bedroom, listening to R.W.Shambauch on the radio. He said, "If you want to be filled with the Holy Ghost with the evidence of speaking in other tongues, lay your hand on this radio in faith as a point of contact." For the first time I heard the words, in Faith. In obedience to the preacher, I laid my hands on that radio, in faith and the Lord filled me with the Holy Ghost and I went to my knees speaking in other tongues.

I'm telling you I felt like a balloon had been blown up inside of me. I looked outside and the trees seemed greener, the sky seemed bluer and everything seemed brighter. I know that doesn't happen to everyone; I just wanted to tell you how it happened to me.

I was so excited that I went to Sandra's house. When she opened the door, I began speaking in tongues. She screamed and shouted and thanked the Lord.

My life has never been the same. The first dramatic change I noticed was the peace and calm that flooded my soul, my mind, my will, my emotions. The next dramatic change was how the Bible came alive to me. I had memorized scripture as a child and could quote it to you by rote. But, for the first time, I actually knew what it meant. I had an insatiable hunger for the Word. I couldn't get enough. I spent approximately eight hours a day studying the Bible for about three months. I was consumed and loving every minute of it.

The one healthy thing this immersion in the Bible did for me was to take my focus off of Ronnie and all of his faults. I had another lover, Christ Jesus. Ronnie was glad for me, but he was so wrapped up in himself and what he wanted to do, he really didn't care.

You see, he was in adultery, doing drugs and having fun. He always prided himself on being able to keep what he was doing from me. Nevertheless, every once in a while, somebody would come to the house and tell on him. Besides, I really didn't want to know.

Now that I was learning so much and growing in the things of God, I began to feel sorry for Ronnie. I said, "Lord, You have got to save Ronnie and fill him with the Holy Ghost." He said to me, "I will save him and fill him and you will have to trot to keep up with him–if you do what I tell you to do."

Praise God! The adventure was on. The Lord said, "Start *calling those things that be not as though they were* (Rom 4:17). Start thanking me that Ronnie Calloway is saved, filled with the Holy Ghost and walking in the light of the Word."

I laughed because Ronnie Calloway was walking around in platform shoes, a wide-brim hat, bell-bottoms with a leather bag hanging over his shoulder. That is the way God operates; I learned that very quickly.

He calls those things that are not as though they were. I stopped nagging and fussing with Ronnie and forgave him. That freed me up to pray for him and to love him.

One morning, he came home about 3:00 a.m., smelling like perfume. I got up out of bed and asked him, "Are you hungry?"

"Yes."

"Can I fix you some breakfast?"

"Yea, fix me some pancakes, steak and eggs."

I did, with no attitude just the love of Jesus in my heart. He didn't know what to think of me. I frankly didn't know what to think of myself. All I knew was it was God loving him through me. Before I was filled with the Spirit, I could I never have done that; but, I was yielded to the Spirit of God.

THE POWER OF GOD

One day, the refrigerator went out and Ronnie had to throw away all the meat in the freezer. I saw that the devil was trying to steal from me; I was not going to have it. I asked Sandra to come over and we laid our hands on that refrigerator and prayed. Don't you know that refrigerator started working again? I thought Ronnie was going to run out in the street screaming. He could not believe his eyes; but, he had to. A few weeks later the dryer stopped working. This time I didn't need Sandra. My faith was so strong that I laid hands on that dryer myself. I commanded that dryer to work in the name of Jesus. It started working and continued to work for at least fifteen more years. Ronnie couldn't deny the reality of the power of God.

God performed several miracles during the next two years. During that time, the Lord wooed Ronnie unto Himself through me. In 1976, Ronnie was saved and filled with the Holy Ghost. And, he lived the life of faith for several years (Romans 2:4). He stopped drinking, smoking, doing drugs, and running around with other women. Ronnie joined the church, read his Bible daily, and lived the way the Word says to live. He became the husband God had promised he would be.

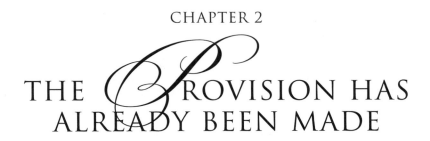

CHAPTER 2

THE PROVISION HAS ALREADY BEEN MADE

In 1982, things changed again. We moved to Marietta, Georgia where most of Ronnie's family lived. We had quite a bit of money from the sale of our house in Denver; so, we didn't look for jobs right away. I believe that set up a mindset of complacency in both of us.

When we did begin our job search, we found it difficult to find work. The pay scale was much less than that in Colorado. Subsequently, we decided to go into the catering business for ourselves. That worked very well, for a while; but when it failed, Ronnie became despondent. All of the fight went out of him.

As the bills increased, we were not able to pay them. Even the house payment was impossible to meet at times. Nevertheless, God was always faithful and more than enough.

At times, I would pray and believe God for finances, go to the mailbox in faith, and find a check from somebody who said we had overpaid them back in Denver. Even though God performed miracle after miracle, our relationship grew more and more strained. Everything became my fault.

Our life became reverted to the period before Ronnie was saved. He began to have a roving eye and lust for other things. One day, we were sitting at the kitchen table and another woman called and asked to speak to him. He tried to tell me some crazy story about who she was, but he was guilty as sin. After arguing about that for awhile, he refused to talk about it any more.

THE BEGINNING OF THE END

A month or so later, he came to me and said he was leaving because we couldn't see eye-to-eye. I told him to go and tell his teenage daughters that he was leaving. Rhonda was devastated and wanted to know what happened to the Christian father he was supposed to be. Chaunci just wanted to know when she would get her child support. After much discussion and drama, he changed his mind. But things were never the same.

I took refuge in the Lord (Psalm 46:1). I knew I was in a place where nobody could take care of my girls and I except God, my father. I immediately recommitted my thought life to Him. I found a job as a receptionist for a small Christian business.

The bookkeeper was a wonderful woman of God who took a liking to me; maybe she just felt sorry for me. I shared with her about our financial situation; she did everything she could to help me. She allowed Rhonda to dust her house, once a week, so that she could have some extra money. You see, it was Rhonda's senior year in high school.

Rhonda very much wanted to go to school in Oklahoma; and, I told her she could. I always raised our girls to *trust the Lord with all their hearts and lean not to their own understanding* (Proverbs 3:5). They knew, from the time they were little girls, *that with God, all things are possible* (Mark 9:23). Somehow Rhonda *knew* she was going to college–even though we couldn't pay the gas and light bills sometimes.

Ronnie finally got a job with the Fulton County Public Schools; however, he was dissatisfied with the meager pay and the work environment. He hated the job.

Soon, Rhonda received a big scholarship which was renewable every year with the work- study program. This was such a blessing; but, it was not quite enough. I remember praying for her day and night and asking God not to let me disappoint her. From the first grade, Rhonda had always been a straight 'A' student. I truly think she is brilliant.

It was now time for her to go to school. But, we didn't even have the gas money to drive her to Oklahoma. Not to mention having nowhere to stay after we got there. I saw it was all on me. Ronnie said he didn't have any money and that was that.

As I was praying one day, the Lord spoke to me and said, "The provision has already been made." I thought, "That's great! But where is the provision?" I found out later, as I meditated on the Word, that the provision is Christ Jesus. As I would continue to believe in Him, everything we needed would manifest. I just began to rest in Him as we continued to make preparations for her to go.

One day, I was sitting at my desk at work when Peg, the bookkeeper, came to me and said, "The Lord told me to give you my credit card. Use it to take Rhonda to school. I want you to put gas in the car and get a hotel room when you need to stop and rest. You just sign my name. If you have any trouble, have them to call me, even if it is 2:00 in the morning. You sign my name in confidence."

That is exactly what I did. Chaunci and I took Rhonda to school and God did the rest. That is the way God wants us to live. Take advantage of the provisions He has made for us through the finished work of Jesus at the cross. Forget not all of His benefits and do it all in confidence in the name of Jesus (Psalm 103:2; 1 John 5:14).

Rhonda graduated with a degree in Telecommunications and Broadcasting on God's miraculous provision. God performed so many miracles that time and space would not allow me to tell them all. There is an old song that says, "He's done so much for me I cannot tell it all." He has, even until this day, been more than enough.

CHAPTER 3

*L*ORD, DID I HEAR YOU CORRECTLY?

few months later, I took a position as administrator of a local ministry. I enjoyed my work... for a year. But then, for some reason, my boss and I were at odds. The conflict grieved me deeply, sometimes God shakes things up to get your attention. I knew it was time for me to go.

In January of nineteen eighty six, after much praying and fasting, the Lord told me He had "created a position" for me in Denver. God said I would make more money than I had ever made. I would be helping people and I would enjoy it more than any job I had ever had. When I told Ronnie about it, he was elated at the prospect of moving back to Denver.

We were not going to move until May when Rhonda came home from her first year of college. We were all excited. But, when it was time for us to pack up and go, Ronnie said, "Jack, I'm not going. I'm going to stay here until the house sells. I don't want it to depreciate due to a lack of care."

Stunned, I said, "You're talking about a house; what about your family?" He assured me that it would be okay, "I am sure it will sell soon. I will be right along, shortly." I prayed about what I should do. One thing I have learned over the years about God is this: when He says it's time to go, it could be dangerous to stay.

Ronnie had started smoking marijuana again. So, the old lifestyle was back as were the frequent bouts of strife and contention. The most I could do was pray. I didn't realize I was in denial. There were so many things I knew in my heart that I didn't want to see or admit. We talked to each other less and less, giving each other the silent treatment. The foundation of our marriage was slowly crumbling. When we did talk, we argued.

One of the things I noticed was the decreasing respect Ronnie had for the girls and me. He was no longer opening the doors, carrying the groceries or lifting the garage door for us. That hurt. It began to erode my self-worth.

Ronnie continued to assure me that it would only take a few weeks for the house to sell. After all, it was a beautiful thirty-two hundred square foot house, sitting on a wooded acre. God had blessed us with that property. Why wouldn't it sell?

Ronnie said again, "I will be with you in Denver within a month."

RONNIE NEEDS TO BE HERE

One of my very close friends in Denver was looking forward to our return; I made arrangements to stay with her. Weeks turned into months while we waited for Ronnie to come; but, he wouldn't come. There was one excuse after another. Over the next year, the girls and I ended up living with four different families.

When we first got to Denver that job God had promised me was no where in sight. I was compelled to *walk by faith and not by sight*. In the meantime, God supernaturally provided a scholarship as well as a very good job for Rhonda. So, she went back to college in Oklahoma. She worked her way through school.

I took a job as a manager trainee at a pizza restaurant; I had to learn every phase of the business. I had to wait tables, make pizza and mop the floor. Everything was fine until I had to lift huge, steel dough bowls and scrub the floor with an industrial-size mop. I pulled something in my abdomen and that was my last night on that job.

My professional background was in the media. I was an on-air radio personality for many years. I produced and hosted a weekly television program on PBS called "Aisha" for over six years. I had always held positions in Denver, not jobs.

Soon after my pizza job, Betty Jones, a long time friend who managed a beauty supply store asked me, "Do you want a job until you can find **the** job?" Thankfully, I said, "I most certainly do." I went to work for her that week.

At the first friend's house where we stayed, we simply wore out our welcome. I did something that upset her and I knew it was time to leave. The next friend was very nice to us, as were they all. But, pretty soon, I knew we had worn out our welcome there too.

I asked my brother if we could stay with him and his wife. They were very nice to us also. But, after about three months, my brother said to me, "Jackie, you and Chaunci will have to find another place to live after Christmas. Ronnie needs to be here or you should be there so he can be responsible for his family."

This was in November and I was crushed. In six months, Chaunci and I had lived with three different families. I felt as though I was living a nightmare. I was trapped in a place where there seemed to be no way out. I didn't have enough money to get my own apartment. I was only making four dollars an hour. Chaunci needed things every week because it was her senior year in high school.

At each house where we had stayed, I tried to be invisible but as helpful as I could. I felt more and more like an outcast. I felt abandoned and betrayed by my husband. It was even deeper than that; I asked myself, "Has our twenty-plus year marriage been worth nothing to him? What about his daughters? These are his biological children, I might add. How could he just leave us out here like this to fend for ourselves with almost no means of support?"

It was horrible. We were emotionally abused by people and battered by circumstances. All the while, we were trying to believe a lying husband and father who was in another state.

ALVA AND BETTY

I do have to stop right here to defend my brother, Jimmy. By asking us to leave, he was trying to force Ronnie to assume the responsibility for his family. I knew that my brother would never hurt my kids or me. He loves us very much and we love him. What my brother didn't know, however, was that another girlfriend had told me that Chaunci and I could come and live with her and her husband if we wanted to.

These friends, Alva and Bobby Tinsley, had lived across the street from us for seventeen years before we moved to Georgia. Our children grew up together, and we had always had a great relationship. They were a God-sent blessing. We lived with the Tinsleys for several months.

My friends, Betty–whom I worked for at a beauty supply store– and Alva, would listen to me, for hours, as I tried to sort out my life. Betty did me a big favor by hiring me. She paid me four dollars an hour, eight hours a day, six days a week. This was much less than I was earning before I moved to Georgia. Nonetheless, I was thankful for every penny.

Both Alva and Betty were so supportive and understanding. Even so, I was ashamed. I was ashamed of being in the state I was in. I was ashamed to tell them the whole truth. I didn't tell them I had been trying to get in touch with Ronnie for a week and he had not returned any of my calls.

Where was he and with whom? When I did finally reach him, he told me the answering machine must be broken. I tried to believe him, but why wouldn't he call his wife and daughters in seven days?

I tried to put up a good front with Betty and Alva, even though I knew they could see right through it. They knew I didn't have much money; moreover, they didn't know I needed shoes.

I remember vividly working at the store in some little, rubber, see-through shoes. I worked in them because they were flat and they were comfortable. That year, it snowed in Denver, Colorado in early fall. You guessed it. I was caught in the snow with rubber shoes on because I didn't have money to buy any leather working shoes. Yes, embarrassed and ashamed is an understatement; however, I continued to pray and to trust God.

CREATING A POSITION

One day, Chaunci and a friend were going out for the evening. The young girl's mother called me to let me know when she would be picking Chaunci up. As we were talking, I said to her, "By the way, I'm looking for a job. So, if you hear of anything, let me know."

She responded, "Oh, that's a coincidence. Our committee, at the United Methodist Church headquarters, is in the process of creating a position for an Associate Council Director." All I heard was "Creating a Position." Those were the *exact* words the Lord had spoken to me before I left Georgia.

To make a long story short, that was my position. God moved, supernaturally, to place me there. The pay and benefits were much more than four dollars an hour; this was a professional position. I had an expense account and a secretary.

I was so thankful and pleased with God, my Father. Again, He was more than enough. That was a miracle position for me. The job description called for a lot of travel. They even sent me to Africa, with all expenses paid. I was so excited.

Meanwhile, Chaunci and I were still living with the Tinsleys. Ronnie called and said he was coming to visit for Christmas. Yes, I did say, *visit*. When he arrived and was unpacking his luggage, I saw two pair of alligator shoes in his bag. One was brown and the other black. I could hardly believe my eyes.

Ronnie stayed with us at the Tinsley's house through Christmas. He promised me he would go back to Georgia, quit his job and come back to Denver in one month. It didn't happen.

CHAPTER 4

*N*O FAINTING SPELLS ALLOWED

*A*fter being in Colorado for over a year–without Ronnie–I took some money I had saved and flew to Georgia. We rented a twenty-four foot U-haul truck, put as many of our things in it as possible, and drove back to Denver. There was so much going on in Georgia at the time, it would fill another book for me to tell you. For whatever reason, Ronnie let some people move into our Georgia home. Consequently, we soon lost that beautiful house. Ronnie and I went back to Denver with our marriage in worse shape than it ever had been.

When Ronnie came to Denver, he was very angry and agitated. He became irritated at the least little thing. I felt as though I was walking on eggshells, trying to keep the peace. I knew he was smoking marijuana; but, I wasn't as familiar with cocaine. That drug causes sudden mood swings which I didn't understand. He was only snorting once in a while, but it sure did make him hard to live with.

I tried to keep Chaunci and Rhonda sheltered from the arguing and the strife; but, they told me they couldn't wait to leave home for college. Knowing they felt that way made me feel horrible, but, I did want them out of harm's way.

Chaunci graduated high school, got an academic scholarship and went to College in Oklahoma with Rhonda.

A few months after Ronnie came to Denver; my job sent me to Atlanta on a business trip. My friend and I took Ronnie's mom and sister to breakfast. I told them how angry Ronnie was with me. No matter what I did, it was never enough. I didn't know what to do to make things better. He seemed to resent the fact that I had a professional position.

His mother said, "Don't let him make you think you're doing anything wrong." She told me that he had another woman there in Georgia while I was in Denver. I was crushed. He had introduced her to our nieces. I was heartbroken. They even told me her name; I had read that name on a card that she sent to our apartment right after he had come back to Denver. I had allowed him to explain it away.

Not only had she sent a card saying, "Thank you for the many hours we spent together. I don't believe you know how much I really do love you." She also sent a Patty LaBelle tape which featured a song, "Somebody Loves You". He tried to explain them away but couldn't. Trying to keep the peace, I just let it go. "Now," I thought, "Here I am, face to face with all of *this* again."

I was so depressed that I stayed in bed and cried for the next three days. I didn't want to believe what I had heard; but, I knew it was true.

Confronting Ronnie would not be easy but on returning to Denver, I did. Ronnie said that everyone was lying. But I had learned to tell when Ronnie was lying…and he was lying.

SHU SHU

I called my best friend, Leslie, who lived in Detroit. I asked if I could come to see her. I needed some personal counseling. I told her what was going on and she said, "Come and stay as long as you want."

In October, I went to Detroit and spent a week with her. It was good for me to be there. We talked day and night. She had some things going on in her life that I addressed and I surely needed her input on what was going on with me.

We affirmed one another. She said something to me that I will never forget. "Remember Jackie, you were somebody before you met Ronnie Calloway." Wow! This was coming from somebody whom I've known since we were three years old. We slept on the same cot in nursery school and wet on each other. As teenagers, we used to polish each others toenails.

"Jackie, you are a very smart person. You have had some super jobs. You love the Lord and He has always taken good care of you." She continued, "You have been in some bad places before, but with God's direction and your mama's love, you have always landed on your feet. Where you are now in your marriage is not the end of the world. You have what it takes to make it through this crisis. You *know* I'll be right here if you need me."

That was all I needed to hear. Her confidence in me helped me to look at my life from a different perspective. I am not a victim but a victor. When I got back to Denver, Leslie called and thanked me for speaking frankly to her about some issues she was going through. She said, "Thank you for being the best friend anyone could ever have."

I said, "No, thank *you*. I love you much."

"Jack, I love you too–like a sister."

Shu Shu, as Leslie was affectionately known, had always been so cute. She was only five feet tall, with beautiful bronze colored skin, a button nose, big, dark, brown eyes and pretty, straight, black hair. When we were kids, I used to covet her two long, thick, silky braids. The most popular girl in school, Shu Shu was outgoing and confident. She was a great dancer and loved to sing. Described by many as the life of the party, her laugh was contagious. Her personality was truly magnetic.

We decided we would go to the Virgin Islands together the following summer just to get away from all of the stress and pain. Shu Shu had taught middle school in the inner city of Detroit for about twenty years and she welcomed any breaks she could get.

About the third week in December, I called Shu Shu and asked her to come to Denver to spend Christmas with us. She said, "Oh no. I'm saving my money to go on our trip to the Virgin Islands this summer. I'm going home to West Virginia for Christmas, where I won't have to spend any money."

"Okay Shu. Thanks again for the good counsel you gave to me in Detroit." She laughed, "I was thinking about you the other day. Thank you, again, for being the best *best* friend anyone could ever have." Huh, that's my buddy.

But…sometimes life doesn't always go as we plan. It certainly didn't for Shu Shu. On Christmas Eve, I received a call that Shu Shu had been shot in Huntington, West Virginia. At that time, Huntington had one of the lowest crime rates in America. I couldn't understand how you could live in Detroit, teach in inner city schools for twenty years and get shot in Huntington…on Christmas Eve?

Shu Shu's mom filled me in on the details: Shu Shu was on her way to Huntington. She was leaving a rest stop when a man shot her. He was trying to car-jack her brand new Volvo. We had picked that car out together during my October stay in Detroit. He shot her in the neck, the chest, and the hand but. By the grace of God, all the bullets entered and exited her body.

She sped away from the gunman and drove until she began to loose consciousness. The blood loss was enormous; nevertheless, she had the presence of mind to park her car crosswise, in the middle of the street, until someone got to her and called an ambulance. She was taken to a nearby hospital, where her wounds were cleaned and patched up

A friend of ours, who is a nurse at the hospital, told me that Shu Shu was sitting up laughing that night. She joked, "I have to get an evening dress with a turtleneck to hide the bullet wounds in my neck. I have a Christmas dance to go to." I said, "That sounds just like her silly self."

Her mom said, "Jackie, she wants you to come and see about her." I said, "Tell her that I will be there as soon as I can get on a plane."

She said, "She'll have surgery to rewire her jaw and her hand at eight in the morning. After that, the doctors will let us know when she can go home."

The next morning, at six o'clock a.m. mountain standard time–eight a.m. in Huntington–I got up to pray for the surgery to go well. When I started praying, I couldn't. My prayers seemed like they were hitting a brick wall. I kept starting and stopping. It was so strange. I couldn't concentrate. Then the phone rang. It was Emma, another close friend of ours in Huntington. Crying, she said, "Jackie, Shu Shu didn't make it."

"What are you talking about?" Emma repeated, "She didn't make it."

"I don't understand what you are saying. She didn't make what?" She exclaimed, "Shu Shu is dead."

That just wouldn't penetrate my brain. I hung up the phone and walked around my house for about an hour just saying, "No, no no no no no no no no no no no. God, no no no no no. This is not happening. No, no! This is not true." I was in shock. I finally woke Ronnie up and said, "Shu Shu is dead."

He was in shock. My girls were in shock. For a long time, I couldn't cry or anything. It just wouldn't penetrate my brain. I found out later that the doctors had killed her during surgery. The doctors were giving her a tracheotomy to revive her. However, they gave her too much anesthetic and punctured her lung. I could not believe it. Again, I was devastated.

In an uncontrolled outburst I cried, "What is going on God? We still haven't found out who shot her or why; now she is dead? No! This is way too much. I never had a chance to talk to her. I never did say goodbye." (Even now as I write this I weep.)

Two days later, the Lord said to me, "I want you to preach the funeral."

"Lord," I said, "You are asking too much. That was my best friend. I want to cry and fall out and let them fan me. You are asking too much." But He said, "There will be people there who need to hear what I want to say through you."

"Lord, they have a preacher at that church. I just can't do this."

I felt so cheated that I didn't have a chance to talk to her. I had so much in me that I wanted to say.

When I got to Huntington, I asked Shu Shu's parents if I could do anything for them. Her father said to me, "Jackie, you know we just got a new preacher at our church. He didn't even know Shu. Bessie and I want to know if you would do the Eulogy. Nobody knew her better than you did."

I wanted to scream, "NO! I can't do this." But I said, "I will do the best I can." I felt guilty that I wasn't with her and that I never had a chance to say goodbye. So, on the flight to Huntington, I wrote this poem to her.

DEAR SHU SHU

Dear Shu Shu this comes from all your friends
who loved and knew you well,
The ones you laughed so hardy with and even secrets you did tell.
We are all here today so sad because you left so soon,
But we have come to say farewell and celebrate in tune.
You're going home to be with God to get your just reward
And hear Him say well done my child He knows the road was hard.
The times you cried and needed help to continue on your way,
He was always there to pick you up and lead you day by day.
When we prepared for 4-H camp and packed our clothes for days,
You always used to help me plan the council circle plays.
We sang on every talent show that they would let us in,
The galaxies, cluster of stars we always knew we'd win.
The football games, the Douglass band, the socials and the cards,
The cigarettes and yes the beer you always partied hard.
You were the life of the party you know, and everyone agreed,
Let's call Shu Shu we know she'll come we never had to plead.
I don't know why you left me here to live without your smiles.
You know last month we laughed and talked and drove together miles.
You said you hoped that we could all survive our mid-life crisis.
I never dreamed you wouldn't stay to help me in my crisis.
For truly it's so hard to stand today and say goodbye,
Because I love you so, so, much and all I do is cry.
But some of these are tears of joy because I know you're safe.

I know you're with our Jesus Christ, The Prince of Peace not hate.
Creator God our Lord Most High, El Elyon is His name,
Has welcomed you with open arms and called you just the same.
So while we're here in Huntington on such a sad occasion,
We'll laugh and share and hug each other a lot with deep compassion.
And Shu we'll never forget you your spirit or your life.
But we'll try hard to love each other and never get in strife.
I'll always see you dancing and swinging to the beat,
Of Teddy, Gladys and all the sounds you loved to move your feet.
I miss you so and always will because you're part of me.
But I'll go on in God I'll trust and will His servant be.
So Shu farewell until that time when we shall meet again
Beyond the galaxies above and just around the bend.
And I'll be strong and teach the children as you did so well,
And tell them of a friend I had, Shu Shu that rings a bell.

EMOTIONALLY DESTROYED

It was standing room only, I did do the best I could do. However, the Holy Spirit really preached that funeral. Then, the school teachers, who worked with Shu Shu, asked me if I would fly to Detroit to preach at a memorial service for her colleagues and students. I did that too.

Because the murder was still unsolved, the media was there at the funeral. They had her case on "America's Most Wanted" television program. Before that dumb surgery, Shu Shu was conscious. So, she was able to give them a perfect description of the gunman. Soon after it aired, his family convinced him to turn himself in. He did.

Finally, the facts were revealed. The gunman had killed his girlfriend in Georgia. In an attempt to complete his get-away, he spotted Shu Shu's nice, new Volvo. He probably thought he could kill her and take the car. She was at the wrong place at the wrong time.

"I have lost my greatest supporter, my confidant," I mourned. "The one person in this world who knew me best is gone." Dealing with the grief over the infidelity in my marriage *and* the grief over Shu Shu, I was emotionally destroyed.

CHAPTER 5

THE *D*EBILITATING DEPRESSION

*F*requently, we are faced with seemingly insurmountable circumstances. Eventually, we can no longer side step nor avoid them; we must conquer them. After coping with all of the anger, hurt, lies, disappointments, arguments, grief, and stress for nearly twenty-five years of marriage, I found myself losing it. The pressure was taking a toll on me.

Ronnie and I could not agree on anything. He would work sometimes and sometimes he wouldn't. I was pretty much taking care of him.

I had to give a presentation at an important meeting at work. As I was introduced, I took the floor, wearing my blue, pinstriped, power suit. Suddenly, I realized that I had forgotten to put on my bra. I wanted to shrink to the floor with embarrassment. I could not believe I didn't put on my bra! What was wrong with me? What was happening to my mind? I had never done anything like that before.

That day, I knew I had to make some changes. I felt as though I was losing my mind. I not only had no control of my emotions, but now my mind and body began to show signs of disarray. This caused me to become very concerned about myself.

Up until then, I was trying to keep everyone else from suffering the effects of a failed marriage. However, I had to face the fact that if I didn't begin to help myself, I might actually lose my mind. Something had to be done.

1 Thessalonians 5:17, *"Pray without ceasing"* became my reality. There were times when I couldn't distinguish whether I was talking to God, to me or to someone else. My constant prayer was, "Lord, show me what to do." I felt the spirit of oppression and the cloak of heaviness all over me. As hard as I tried to ignore it, keep moving and go on with my daily routine, it got worse and worse. Sometime, I just wanted to sleep. It was more and more difficult to get out of bed in the mornings. Everyday, I fought to get my head off the pillow. I had to keep telling myself to put one foot in front of the other.

I loved my job. I interacted with people all day. However, I had to show up and I had to perform. So, I couldn't crack up! Also, my girls were away in college and already concerned about me. I couldn't let them down by having a nervous breakdown; they were counting on me to encourage them and to send them money.

Yes, I became the sole provider. Yet there was no appreciation. Instead, Ronnie told me I thought I was something because I had that job. I would come home from work and Ronnie would be coming off the golf course. He would contribute a hundred dollars here and there–now and then. But, the rest was up to me. However, I must say that God did provide financially.

Ronnie and I were constantly arguing. He was doing drugs and running around while I was trying to stay away from home, as much as possible. Whenever my job wanted me to travel out of town, I was glad to go. I hated being in the same house with him.

"WHAT AM I SUPPOSED TO DO?"
In June of that year, my job sent me to a week-long conference in Fort Collins, Colorado. I thought about my miserable life every single day.

When I left the conference, I started my drive home in a daze. A sense of dread engulfed my heart. The last thing I wanted to do was to see Ronnie–to walk back into that emotionally abusive atmosphere. When I entered Aurora, Colorado I drove into my girlfriend's apartment complex. I proceeded past her apartment to the leasing office. I told the manager that I was interested in leasing a two-bedroom apartment.

I could not believe I was doing this. I didn't even know if I could rent an apartment. After losing that house in Georgia, our credit was so bad. Ronnie had paid no bills. Even though I was doing the best I could, sometimes things were still paid late.

As the manager was showing me the apartment, I was walking behind her thinking, "Lord, what am I doing?" He responded, "All lights are green until you see a red."

"But Lord, I don't want a divorce. I love Ronnie. I want my marriage to work. What am I doing?" The manager interrupted, "Do you like this one?"

"Oh, Yes I do. This is very nice." We went back to the office and I filled out some papers. Then she asked, "Will I find anything on your credit?"

"Yes, you probably will. I am leaving my husband. One of the reasons is because he hasn't kept a job for the last two years. Consequently, we have had some financial difficulties." She responded, "Because you were honest with me, I will only check *your* credit. We will let you know tomorrow if we can receive you as a resident or not." I thanked her and left.

I prayed, "Now Lord, if I'm not supposed to do this, the credit check won't be favorable. I'll just wait for further instructions." The next day, the manager called me, "Mrs. Calloway your credit is "A" number one. We would love to have you as a resident. You can move in on the first of the month."

Ronnie was furious when I told him I was leaving him and moving out of the house we were renting. "And just what am I supposed to do?"

"Just whatever you want to do," I replied. "I'm sure some of those women you have been with will be glad to let you live with them. All I know is I am tired of taking care of a grown man who wants to talk to me crazy and treat me like I'm such a hassle to be around. I'm leaving before I lose my mind. You know our marriage is over and has been for a long time. You still refuse to admit that you've been with other women, so we can't even begin to try to make things better."

"No Jack. You just want to believe everybody else except me."

"Yea, everybody like your own mother and sister…not to mention the woman who sent that card here saying how much she still loves you and thanks you for the many hours you spent with her in Atlanta…all while the girls and I were here struggling. You are absolutely right. I refuse to believe you anymore. I've heard enough lies."

A DOWNWARD SPIRAL

I finally left Ronnie. Surprisingly, he was nice enough to help me move. As I settled in my new apartment, I was thankful for the peace and quiet. I didn't have to argue every night anymore. I was no longer looked at with disgust and disdain every morning. However, I was faced with the fact that my marriage had failed.

I thought to myself, "Jackie you are now a statistic. How could this have happened to you? You said you would never get a divorce. You don't believe in divorce." I had to believe that somehow, Ronnie would come to his senses and we would get back together again. Nonetheless, I sank deeper and deeper into a paralyzing state of depression. The more I thought about all of the years I had sacrificed for Ronnie, the worse I got. I had gladly given him all of my youth, in total faith and confidence. I cried every day.

For all of those years, I had worked different jobs because he wanted me to. He wanted the money for all the things he thought he had to have: a new car, new furniture, clothes, and golf vacations. It seemed as if I had lived most of my life for him. Now, I had been trashed. Don't get me wrong. In all fairness to Ronnie, prior to the last several years, he always worked. We worked together. That's why I couldn't understand the drastic change in him.

What about his girls? How could he treat his own children like this? He had always been the Super Dad who took them to Disneyland and

Disneyworld and rode on all the rides with them. As they got older, he took them on dates–together and separately–to teach them how a man should treat them. He opened the doors for them, held their chairs, and told them never to settle for less than the best in a man or in life. Now where was he?

In reality, the greatest thing a father can do for his children is to love God first and then their mother. When they see and experience that love and the atmosphere it creates, it can mold their character and give them their God intended identity. Our children can be taught at home how to be godly fathers, husbands, mothers and wives. Home is their first classroom and we their first teachers.

WHY?

I cried day and night until I had no more tears left…and then I cried some more. I became even more despondent as I asked God the question, "Why? Why did Ronnie have to have other women? Why couldn't he have remained faithful to You God, and to me? What was wrong with me? Was I so ugly and undesirable?" In spite of all the truth I knew, my self-esteem plummeted.

While searching for answers to those questions, I reflected on my childhood in West Virginia. My mother instilled in me that I should look my best, everyday. As a result of that training, I consistently kept up my physical appearance. I didn't get fat after having my children. I didn't even get fat after having an emergency hysterectomy when I was twenty-six years old. I only weigh one hundred and thirty pounds now. I've definitely kept my hair and clothes nice. I've never been a big spender, always looked for the bargains. I love our children and raised them *in the nurture and admonition of the Lord* (Ephesians 6:4). I sacrificed what **I** wanted or needed for what was best for them. I didn't understand what was wrong with me and why this had to happen.

The more I questioned myself, the foggier my thinking became. "Lord, talk to me. Why did You let this happen? Does this faith stuff really work? Why, God, Why?"

CHAPTER 6

IT WAS ALL A FAÇADE

A was still trying to work that wonderful job for the United Methodist Headquarters. The Lord had created that position for me. However, it was getting more and more difficult to wear the mask. But I continued to wear it well.

It was almost like being a talk show host again. In the nineteen seventies I produced and hosted a television broadcast on PBS for about six years. There I learned to get everything ready behind the scenes and then sit down in front of the camera, smile and, "Go to Hollywood." I would say, "Hi I'm Jackie Calloway and welcome to Aisha." My real life had the same feel as *let's pretend*. Let's pretend the world is great and I'm happy, strong and successful. It was all a façade.

I managed to keep up appearances for quite sometime, but I was becoming more and more lonely. I missed Ronnie every single day. I didn't know how to be alone. What do you do if you are not coming home cooking dinner, while making conversation or arguing with the person you had been *one* with for more than twenty years? I was miserable.

Then late one night there was a knock on my door. As a matter of fact the date was August twenty seventh, our wedding anniversary. I opened the door and there was Ronnie Calloway with a bouquet of flowers and a beautiful card. To tell the truth I was glad to see him. He handed me the flowers and asked if he could come in. I said, "Yes."

"Thank you for the flowers and what exactly are they for?" He asked me to read the card. It was an anniversary card and it said how much he loved and needed me. "I apologize to you, Jackie, for all I have done in the past to hurt you. Please forgive me and let's make up. I've been so wrong and I know it, but I want us to start all over again so I can make things right."

At that point I was so lonely, depressed, weak, and hot that I embraced him. We kissed, and I opened my heart and everything else to him again. I allowed him to spend the night, and the next day he got his things and moved in with me.

Our daughters, who were home from college for the summer at the time, could not believe I took Dad back. I really couldn't believe it myself. We had about a week of fun and romance because we didn't discuss anything that was important. When we started talking about who was going to pay what, and with what, the tension returned. Needless to say, in two weeks our relationship was worse than before. After a few months of misery, I almost had enough, again.

Once again Ronnie was not working. He had been fired. The van he drove was one I had purchased at my credit union a year earlier. He told me he was not going to make the payment on the van that month. That made me so angry because he knew the account was in my name. I had to make the payment.

One morning I didn't go to work and the phone rang; it was another woman on the line for Ronnie. I thought okay, enough is enough. Here we are right back in the same miserable place. I couldn't get him to move out so I moved again into a one-bedroom apartment.

I knew I had done everything I could do to make this marriage work, including prayer and fasting. I wanted more than anything to do the right thing, but with no cooperation and much disrespect it became impossible for me.

The good thing *about* all of this was that *God was supplying all my need according to His riches in glory by Christ Jesus* (Philippians 4:19). Financially I was doing well because I trusted the Lord. He showed me how to pay off all of the bills. They were mainly credit card debts that Ronnie had promised to pay and didn't.

As I prayed and asked the Lord to show me how to become debt free, He did. One night He woke me up and told me to borrow the total amount I owed on the cards from my credit union at a much lower interest rate. Have the credit union take the payments out of my check, and I would never miss the money. That is exactly what I did, and in less than a year I was totally debt free. I am a firm believer in the scripture in Deuteronomy 28:12b where we are promised that *you shall lend to many nations, but you shall not borrow.* However, many times because we have sinned, by ignoring God's instructions, we reap the opposite of God's promises.

Several months passed and I still could not get over my whole life being turned upside down. I kept going through the motions of living my life, but I just couldn't shake the feeling of failure. I could not believe that all of the praying, hoping, and trusting in God for Ronnie to change had gone for naught.

I was so lonely yet all I could think of was Ronnie, and how our marriage should not have come to this. I hadn't heard from Ronnie for some weeks. I decided to call him. He was staying with his aunt here in town.

As I dialed the number I tried to brace myself for his anger. "Hello, how are you doing?" He responded solemnly, "I'm fine how 'bout you?"

"I'm doing okay."

"So, why are you calling me?"

"I'm calling because I miss you Ronnie, and I want to know why don't you get yourself together and do the right thing so we can be together?"

"Jack, you are the one who put me out, so why are you calling me now?"

"Ronnie you know that all you have to do is repent and surrender your life to the Lord again and He will make our marriage work."

"I confessed to you already and told you I didn't have intercourse with anybody, but you won't believe that. I have to go now and I'll talk to you later." He hung up the phone.

Each time I talked to him the conversation ended like that. It made me sad and depressed. Ironically, I began to turn my frustrations toward God. "God, why didn't you make Ronnie do the right thing? What was it I was doing wrong God that you didn't answer my prayers? I trusted You for my marriage and you let me down." From that time on, I began to spiral down deeper into depression.

My job required a lot of travel; consequently I spent many lonely nights in hotel rooms across the country. I began to have a glass of wine with my lunch and dinner every day. Then pretty soon I began to buy myself a bottle of wine and take it to my room. I saw that if I drank, I would sleep and not have to lie awake thinking about what a failure I was, and why I wasn't woman enough to keep my husband.

Once while having lunch in San Francisco by the Bay it dawned on me that it was Ronnie's birthday. I wondered where he was and what was he doing on his birthday. I could hardly eat for crying. I left the restaurant, walked along the Bay and met a sweet white-haired couple who were fishing. They asked how are you doing and I began to cry all over again. They both rushed to comfort me. I told them I thought I would be fishing with my husband in our old age but he had chosen to be with someone else. The old gentleman said, "Well he is crazy because you are a pretty lady." That didn't help me much but I will never forget the encounter.

CHAPTER 7

THE $\mathcal{L}$OVES I LOST

$\mathcal{I}$ was smart enough to know that I should not spend the holidays alone but always with friends who cared about me. Those friends who cared about me most were in Huntington. My mom had moved from there when my father died several years earlier, but I had some friends there who were closer to me than some of my blood kin. These are friends I grew up with. So, every Christmas I would go to West Virginia and we would party.

In my experience, few of us are blessed with a safe place where we can take off our masks and come out of our costumes. We long for a place of sincere validation, where we are welcomed and celebrated for just being you. All I had to do in this place was show up, receive and give love. That's how it was at home.

We would sit for hours and reminisce about old times. We listened to all the oldies but goodies–the songs from the fifties and sixties that we grew up dancing to at the sock hops and parties. We remembered the silly things we did at 4-H camp, the football games, and the Fredrick Douglass High School band events. We talked of our friends and those great growing up years, while listening to Babyface sing, "I'm never keep'n secrets and I'm never tellin' lies." During Christmas and New Years, our nights wouldn't end until three or four o'clock in the morning.

While my buddies drank brandy with beer to chase it, I would down at least a bottle of champagne…all by myself. But for that little while, I would not think about my whole life being turned upside down. That, I guess, was the whole point. Don't think about reality. This escapism would go on for at least a week.

Sometimes, I would begin to talk about Ronnie and how dirty he did me. I knew that one of these days he was really going to miss me. I just kept wondering what else he wanted in a woman? He probably wanted a woman who didn't talk about God all the time. Maybe he wanted someone who wore tight dresses and went to rock concerts or something. I don't know what he wanted; but, evidently it wasn't me. I think he always had another woman while he was married to me. I don't know; I was just confused.

My friends always made me feel special. That was the good thing about being home. They always told me that they loved me and hugged me all the time. It was a safe haven, except for the drinking. I didn't realize I was becoming addicted to the alcohol; that became a big problem.

LILLIE SMITH

One Christmas, I decided to go to Michigan and spend two weeks with my mom. I couldn't wait to see her and to receive her reassurance and love. My mother and I have always had the greatest relationship in the world. She was strict on us growing up; we knew it was only because she loved us and wanted to protect us in anyway she could.

Mama is a beautiful woman. She gave birth to me when she was forty years old. My younger brother, Michael, was born five years later. He was her ninth child. She bore five boys and four girls. Mama didn't loose that baby fat for many years, but she remained beautiful to me. My mom would be considered a high yellow, African-American woman. She had very fair skin with a few freckles and soft light brown eyes. I got my height from her; she is five feet eight inches tall. Mama has long fingers and beautiful hands. Lillie Smith also has the prettiest crown of silver hair that you have ever seen. I said years ago, "If my hair would gray like Mama's, I will never dye it," and it has.

Mama had this unique sense of humor. She can look you right in the face and say something so funny. You would fall on the floor laughing but she would only smile. Once we were in church and she whispered to me, "That man's after shave is so loud, I can hardly hear the preacher." Well, I laughed so much I almost strangled. She acted like she didn't know what was wrong. She continued to look straight ahead, not cracking a smile.

When I was a teenager, in the fifties and sixties, Mama would get up with us in the living room and dance to the music we were playing. She liked Motown music as much as we did. She loved God from the depths of her heart and was a great example before us, but she knew how to play as well. My mom wasn't a touchy feely person; but, she was right there with us.

I have always loved my mother, deeply. I have the highest respect for her. So much so that I used to pray and ask God to let me die before she did. I didn't think I could bear losing her. When I was in my twenties, I wrote the poem on the next page to honor her on Mother's Day. This poem gives you a vivid picture of how I saw Mama when I was a child.

"WHAT?"

I really wanted to see my mother this particular Christmas. Like a little child, my heart skipped a couple of beats with excitement. As I arrived in Lansing, Michigan, I was speeding in anticipation of my reunion with Mama. It was a sunny but cold day. There were small mounds of dirty snow shoveled on either side of the street. In Denver, it snows and then the sun comes out and melts the snow. Dirty snow is an uncommon sight for me. But this trip was not about Michigan or the snow; I came to see my Mama.

"MAMA"

*Let's look back a moment children, to the days of our childhood,
when life seemed oh so simple, and living it was good.*

*I awoke each morning to the sound of Mama in the kitchen, trying
to start us on our way our breakfast she was fixin'.*

*To see her face when I came down would start my day off right, she
didn't have to smile you see her face gave off a light.*

*It was then her task to see us off to school that we might learn, to
read and write to get a job, a better life to earn.*

*But then upon returning from school each day we'd meet, the aroma
of some oxtail stew and hopefully pig feet.*

*Mama didn't go to high school but to work and had no choice but
to help her deserted mother and be sensitive to her voice.*

*But Mama knew the secret to living life you see. Seek ye first the
kingdom of God she used to say to me.*

*Be kind to all your brothers even strangers you shall meet. Have
hate in your heart for no one, or yourself you will defeat.*

*So by those very standards I've come a long long way, and thanking
God for Mama each and every day.*

*So if your mother is today alive and by your side, show her the love
within your heart, your affections you should not hide.*

*For soon it may be oh too late for all of us to say, "I love you Mama
and hope you have a glorious Mother's Day."*

As I drove into the parking lot of the Senior Citizen's complex where she lived, she waved to me from her balcony and turned swiftly to go inside to press the buzzer, to let me in. She had been looking out of the window and anticipating my arrival as well.

When I finally got inside, she was so glad to see me. We embraced and she told me how good I looked. That was some of what I had come for. The first thing she wanted to know was, "Are you hungry?" She had dinner ready for me with all of my favorites–at the time–macaroni and cheese, candied yams, mustard greens, chitterlings, and a coconut cake.

We laughed and talked. Then, she asked about Ronnie. She always loved Ronnie. But, when he mistreated me, she didn't have much to say to him. After we talked a while, I called my oldest daughter, Margo, on the phone. She also lived in Lansing. While we were talking mama said, "Who is that crazy person you are talking to?" I was stunned.

I asked in disbelief, "Crazy person? Why did you say that?"

"They have to be crazy if they are talking to you." I was floored. For her to call anybody crazy was so out of character for Mama. Then she said, "You need to get off of my phone–running up the bill–before they turn it off." Totally confused at this point I asked, "What are you talking about? Mama, this is Margo on the phone. It's not long distance." I was very puzzled. But she laughed it off and went to another room.

That evening I talked to my sisters. They told me that Mama had been acting very strange and saying some very hurtful things to them also. They said they thought she was showing signs of dementia. Why hadn't I heard this on the phone in my conversations with her? Why hadn't anyone told me this before?

The next day, I noticed a couple of things that she didn't remember. I thought it was odd but, after all, she was over eighty years old. Some memory loss is to be expected. That night, I opened the hide-a-bed in the living room as I had done many times before. After she had gone to bed, I lay there watching television. She came in the living room and stood over me, "You are going to have to get out of here."

"What?"

She sternly said, "How do you expect me to go to sleep knowing **you** are in here?" I was in complete shock. What in the world was wrong with Mama? For a moment, fear gripped me. My first impulse was to cry. Mama had never talked to me like that. I really didn't know what to do.

I calmly said, "Okay, Mama. Just let me sleep here tonight and I will leave tomorrow." That seemed to satisfy her. She went back in her room, turned the light off and went to sleep.

Needless to say, I didn't sleep all night. I lay there, frightened, and silently crying. I could not believe that Mama didn't want me in her house. I did not know what dementia was, consequently, I surely didn't know it could dramatically change a person over night.

I felt frightened, like a three-year-old who didn't know where her Mama was. I really **didn't** know where my Mama was. I prayed, "Oh God please don't let this be happening to Mama. Not now, Lord, when I need Mama so much. God, my whole life is in chaos. What is going on? God please let Mama be all right in the morning. I can't loose her too." Some time before daybreak, I cried myself to sleep.

When I woke up, Mama was in the kitchen cooking breakfast. She looked at me and said, "Good morning. Are you going to sleep all day? You should get up and eat something. Get your clothes on before your sisters and brothers come over here to see you and you won't be dressed."

"Okay I will. How do you feel this morning?"

"I feel just fine. How do you feel?" I answered quickly, "I feel absolutely superb. I'm blessed."

I got up, took a shower, had breakfast with her, and she acted as if last night never happened. We laughed and talked as we always do. My sisters and brothers came to see me as they always do. When they left I said to her, "Mama, you need some things from the store. Do you want me to go and get what you need?"

She said to me sharply, "I'm not giving you my money. That is all you want from me anyway is my money."

"Mama, you know I don't want your money. I give **you** money all the time." She snapped, "You ain't never gave me no money. You're always trying to take mine." I calmly said to her, "Well, I'm going to the store and I will be back soon."

I left that apartment crying. I went to Michael's house and told him what was going on. He said, "Jackie, she has been acting like that for a while now."

"Why hasn't anybody told me about this before now? I can't believe she is over there by herself like that. She is going in and out of reality and nobody is doing anything about it."

"What are we going to do about it?" Michael said, "I think she is getting Alzheimer's disease." Although I didn't want to hear that, I knew something was happening.

Later that evening, I went back to Mama's apartment. As we got ready for bed again, she told me, "Willie doesn't want anybody sleeping on that couch." Now, Willie is my daddy who had been dead for about twelve years. I told her, "He won't mind if I sleep on it one more night. Tomorrow I am going to West Virginia. I promise I won't sleep on it any more." She reluctantly said, "Okay."

Again, I cried myself to sleep. I convulsed with deep, deep sobs into my pillow. When I would lie on my back, the tears wet my hair from my temples to the back of my head. I had begun to mourn the loss of my mother.

The next day, I told Mama, "I love you with all my heart." I hugged her real tight and she hugged me back real tight. I kissed her, got in the car, and began to drive to West Virginia seeking the comfort of my friends.

I NEED SOME CHAMPAGNE

As I left Lansing, I cried uncontrollably. I knew, as I drove and cried, that some day I would write about this. The grief I experienced was almost too heavy to bear. My emotions were out of control. Tears filled my eyes until I could hardly see the road. I cried out loud and my body shook. I yelled, "Mama, Mama, Mama, Oh God, what has happened to Mama? God, God, God please don't let this be happening to Mama. God she is too good. God, all of my life…all I have ever known her to do is love and serve You and teach us about You. Why would You let this happen to Mama?" I literally drove and cried for over four hundred miles, all the way to Huntington.

As I came off the highway into Huntington, I exited onto Hal Greer Boulevard. Years ago, Hal Greer played professional basketball for the Philadelphia 76ers. I thought about him so strongly at **this** time when I saw the street sign. He was one of my brother, George's, best friends, growing up. He had slept at our house on many occasions. Mama had fed him so many meals. I wondered what he would think if he knew that she is no longer in her right mind.

I traveled on cobblestone streets, past Fredrick Douglass High School. During the days of segregation, all the African American teenagers had to attend that school. I thought of the fun high school marching band trips Mama chaperoned while I was a majorette there. It was so sad for me to come home and realize Mama would no longer remember the wonderful moments we shared there.

At last, I turned onto Tenth Avenue. I slowed down as I drove past our old house. I imagined Mama sitting on the front porch. It was over-whelming to think of the years we sat and talked in the swing together on that porch. I don't have the time or the strength to tell you of all the wisdom that she imparted to us at that house. I weep even as I pen these words.

Ironically, my friends Jenny and John live on Tenth Avenue also. The sun was beginning to set, in a beautiful clear sky, when I reached their house. Jenny took one look at my face and knew something was wrong. I told her we had to get some champagne so that I could sit down and tell her what happened. Jenny, John, and Jenny's sister, Beverly, were all very concerned about me.

We got the champagne and I began to talk and cry all over again. They knew how close I was to Mama. They were as grieved as I was, especially after we had had a few drinks. In my experience, when you have a few drinks, if you are happy, you get happier; if you are sad, you get sadder. We all got sadder.

I talked and cried until I was loaded and exhausted. After all, I had driven over four hundred miles from Michigan and had drunk as much

THE Loves I Lost

as I could in a short period of time. I had done what it took to be exhausted so I went to bed.

I want you to know, right now, even though we were all loaded and asleep, we loved each other. Beverly and Jenny asked me several times a day, "Are you all right?"

I'd tell them, "Yes, I'm fine." Then Beverly would say, "Jackie, I love you."

Understand this: although we drank and partied together, we all were church members. But, I didn't have any friends in the church or pastors telling me they loved me as often as Beverly did. It wasn't just me. She had developed a habit of telling people she loved them. Little did she know how much I needed to hear that somebody loved me. It was just God loving me through her.

CAN YOU BELIEVE THAT?

Beverly and I were classmates from the first through the twelfth grades. Ours was not a casual acquaintance. Beverly and Jenny were like sisters to me. But, the worst thing happened in nineteen ninety-nine. **Beverly died**. Can you believe that? Her brother, T.J., called one night to tell me she died. I still can't believe she is gone. Her doctors said she had some rare bone disease that no one ever detected and **she died**. She left behind three beautiful daughters and grandbabies…but my good friend **Beverly died**.

As I am writing this, I'm weeping again. When I think of all of the loss in my life, I'm reminded of all of the wonderful people God has allowed me to know. Bobby Murrell, who grew up across the street from us, was another close friend who was like a brother to me. When we were kids, he would always ask me, "When are you going to marry me?" I'd tell him never and don't touch me; but, I loved him with all of my heart. He died during that same period of time. His doctors said his heart exploded.

About a month before that happened, I was in Huntington to attend the funeral of another close friend, Donnie Spotts. After the funeral, I had the strong urge to go see Bobby. When I arrived at his house, his daughter said he was asleep. I told her to, "Go wake him up and tell him to brush his teeth and come down here to see me right now." He did just that. We laughed and talked for hours. We told each other, I love you, as we had done for years. I never saw him alive again. I will forever be grateful for that time we spent together.

These people genuinely cared about me. They told me and showed me how much they loved me. I believe, as others do, that a true friend is one who learns your song and sings it back to you. When you have those kinds of friends, it makes for an extraordinary life.

There are so many people who go through life and are never affirmed. Some are never encouraged to make their dreams come true. That certainly is not the case for me.

I realize that I have jumped from one subject to another; but, I have to make you understand the true friends I had there in West Virginia. Beverly and Jenny, among others, were there for me when I really needed them. They opened their hearts and homes wide to me. They allowed me to be their sister, kinfolk. They let me see their flaws while they knew all of my shortcomings. They loved me any way while I certainly loved them back.

Many times, we are quick to judge one another, looking at the outside and never taking the time to know the heart. I have known no greater people in this world than Beverly, Jenny and John, Jenny's husband. They were true friends to me. I believe God planned it so. It was just Him loving me through them. I hope you get the picture of true friendship with no strings attached.

Later when I woke up, I was ready for some more champagne. I didn't want to think about Mama or anything sad anymore. I wanted to listen to the music, laugh and dance. Yes, I said dance.

One of our favorite pastimes, growing up in Huntington, was singing and dancing. You might think that's typical for African Americans. Regardless of what you think, that pastime kept many of us out of trouble and gave us something to dream about. My older brother, George, and his singing group actually went to New York and were contestants at the Apollo Theater. Of course, they almost starved to death, but that's neither here nor there. They realized their dream.

I wanted to sing. Beverly put on the music and we began to dance in the living room. We were doing the dog, the calypso, the twist, and singing to the music. I was trying to drown my thoughts. I did a pretty good job of it too. But, I knew that soon, I would again be alone with my fears and grief. But, for that week of Christmas, we had a great time.

CHAPTER 8

WHATEVER EVER HAPPENED TO JACKIE?

'm in Denver; the holidays are over and I'm back on my job trying to maintain a normal life. I had more on my mind than I was able to handle. I was walking around, going through the motions, doing what was necessary for me to keep my head emotionally above water.

Whenever I talked to Mama on the phone, she was forgetting more and more of the important things: those wonderful memories of daddy we used to laugh about every time we were together; those funny things folks use to say and do in the country when she was a little girl. Soon she remembered none of that. I would have phone conversations with her, hang up the phone and cry. She was getting increasingly worse.

Because I needed to be consoled, I thought more and more about Ronnie. I got reports, from time to time, about his changed life.

Someone saw him at a club or somewhere. He had totally changed his lifestyle from a saved, filled-with-the-Holy Ghost example, to conforming to the image of the world. He had become mister man about town. Who was I to talk?

I felt like such a failure. My shame of divorce seemed like something I would never be able shake. Years ago, I saw a billboard that read, "No **success** can ever compensate for **failure** in the home." I never forgot that statement and those words haunted me. As much as I tried, as much as I prayed, as much as I worked on it, my marriage had failed.

I slipped back into depression. If the truth were told, it never left. To mask it, I trained myself to look good on the outside while I was dying on the inside. I felt so sorry for myself. I couldn't let any one know how serious the depression really was. I didn't want to live anymore.

My job required me to be up and active. Each week, I conducted workshops, spoke at churches, did diversity training and attended meetings. It became increasingly hard for me to pay attention to what seemed trivial at work, compared to the darkness overtaking my personal life.

I never stopped believing in God. But, I had lost the strength to exercise my faith. I read the Bible less and less because I wanted to drink more and more. That way, I would not have to think. I did a full day's work and never went to work after drinking. Every day, I looked forward to going home. Most days, I stopped at the liquor store and got me a bottle or two of champagne. Then, I went home and drank one whole bottle and slept.

Along with drinking, I also started smoking cigarettes, which God had delivered me from cold turkey back in nineteen seventy-four. I was hurting so much. I have come to know that oppressive spirits come to take you captive when you open the door to them through grief, self-pity, anger and hurt. James 4:17 says, "*Therefore to him that knoweth to do good, and doeth it not, to him it is sin.*" I also knew that, "*the wages of sin is death; but the gift of God is eternal life through Jesus Christ our Lord*" (Romans 6:23).

I knew the truth and I was willfully turning from it. The sad part is that once you've opened the door to sin, you can't control all that comes in with it. You let in the sin *and* the consequences. It is impossible to get those demonic forces to leave without the power of the Holy Spirit.

I would like to be able to say I called on the Spirit of God and walked free right then, but that is not the case. I continued to drink, more and more. I became angrier. Part of that anger was just the symptom from the guilt I was feeling. Here I was saved, filled with the Holy Ghost and drunk.

Grieving is a process. But if you don't continue to walk through that process, you can get stuck in one of the stages of grief, and never get out. It can be shock, hurt, guilt, or anger. I did get stuck in hurt and guilt for much too long. I stayed in that place of hurt and self pity until I almost grieved myself to death. That does happen you know. More people than death certificates record die of a broken heart.

Then, I moved to that place of "if only" and "what if?" I didn't want to think anymore so I drank and went to sleep for about two years. Drunkenness is a form of sleep. My body became addicted to the alcohol. Whenever I was around someone who had some marijuana, I would smoke that too. I had also started to masturbate; that, to me, was the bottom of the pit. Whatever happened to Jackie? I remember asking myself who are you, really? I was living a double life. The devil was so pleased at my demise. He would say to me, "Look at you. You're just a lousy drunk. What would your girls think of their sweet mother now?"

I cried out, "God please help me. I am so sorry God. How did I ever get here?" Then, the enemy said, "God doesn't hear you when you're like this. You keep saying you're sorry but you keep on doing it again. He knows your heart and He is not buying it."

I stopped socializing with my friends and isolated myself in my apartment. All I wanted to do was be at home with some Luther Vandross music, drink, smoke and cry. Interestingly enough, I was still functional. I still went to work. I still talked to my daughters and friends but I did not talk long and I did not invite them to my apartment often.

The thing about depression and secrets is the devil is able to take full control, causing you to quickly spiral and do some things you never dreamed you would do. I was so lonely and vulnerable. It has been written, "You are only as sick as your secrets."

CHAPTER 9

POURING OUT THE

Poison

One of the by-products of guilt is anger. I became very angry at myself–because of what I'd become–and it showed up on my job. I would be in meetings and someone would make a statement. If it sounded racist or unfair, I lashed out at them with a fury–not cursing, just letting everyone at the table know I didn't like what was said.

After one of those episodes, I told my boss, "I think I need some time off."

"I think you do too. We won't give you a paid leave of absence unless you agree to get counseling."

"*Counseling?*"

"Yes, that will have to be the agreement." I thought for a moment, "I'm single now; I can't afford to be off my job without pay." Although

55

I was determined not to go to a Christian counselor, reluctantly I agreed to go to someone.

Some of what I was experiencing was menopausal symptoms. I went to my doctor for a physical. She referred me to her psychologist, whom she highly recommended. The next day, I called and made an appointment with him. "At least he's not a Christian counselor," I thought. "I know the Word myself." Yet, I wasn't obeying it. I didn't want anyone beating me over the head about my sins, making me feel worse than I already did. I was a self -righteous, prideful in my sins disaster.

When I arrived at the psychologist's office, I took one look at him and knew I was in trouble. I asked him if he had ever counseled a black woman before. "No," he said. "As a matter of fact, you're my first."

"I guess now I have to validate you before I can get counseling for myself." I thought, "What can a white, mountain-looking man tell me about me?" I was truly frustrated.

"Just begin to tell me about you. Why are you here?"

Reluctantly again, I began my story. I was angrier than I knew. It is amazing how God has created us with the capacity to keep walking and doing those things that are necessary for us to survive; all the while, there is a time bomb about to explode on the inside of us.

THE ROOT

I told him all about my twenty plus year marriage, the break up, and why it happened. Over the next several weeks, he delved more deeply into who I am and where I came from. I discovered that much of my anger and behavior stemmed from my childhood.

Growing up in West Virginia during the fifties and sixties, I was confronted with racism on a daily basis. At that time, we were seldom able to speak our minds or have a bad attitude for fear of reprisal on our families or ourselves.

During periods of conflict and racial tension, some of the most valuable people to have in your camp are visionaries. I thought it was wonderful growing up and going to all black schools. We had a very supportive and loving community of people, visionary teachers included. Our teachers knew our potential and demanded that we reach it. They pushed us, with love, beyond what we knew we could do.

To my knowledge, all of the blacks lived in one segregated area. Outside of the Fifteenth Street to Twentieth Street–area especially at night–could be dangerous. You just didn't always know what you would run into. That was my experience.

I loved Fredrick Douglass High School. It was actually a junior and senior high school combined. The grades went from seventh to the twelfth. When I was in the ninth grade, Mr. Simpson, the band director, picked me to be a majorette. I thought I had died and gone to Heaven. We had one of the best marching bands in the state. It was an honor to have been chosen, particularly as a ninth grader. The other majorettes were juniors and seniors.

In nineteen sixty-one, the schools were desegregated and Douglass High School was closed. I thought I had died again, but this time gone to hell. The front page of the newspaper read, "Douglass High School Closed!" I read it and went back to bed and slept all day. I was so sick.

Black students were made to go to all white, Huntington High School. Each morning, we had to walk past Douglass to get to Huntington High. There were so few of us, compared to them, we could never make a difference. The band club representative told me not to waste my time going out for majorette because there would be no black legs marching in front of their band. I was crushed again.

As we continued to try to make the adjustment, we were overwhelmed with the loss of our confidence on a daily basis. The reality was that we had to stay there, whether they wanted us to or not. My world history teacher told me she wasn't answering any of my questions. She said, "We don't want you down here anyway. So, you either get it or you don't." I could not believe it.

One day, as we came to the blond, brick building where most of us entered the school, we saw "F#!$ all you black niggers" painted on the side of the building. They had spelled the "F" word out in dark green paint. That did it for me.

I went home that day and told Mama I was quitting school. To my surprise, she laughed until she cried, "Don't you know that is exactly what they want you to do? Then you would be all of those things they say we are now. If I were you, I would study and do the very best I can and make them out to be wrong. Prove to **yourself** you can do it, even with the opposition."

I thought about it and I said, "You're right. I'm going to finish in the upper third of my class." In nineteen sixty four, by the grace of God, I accomplished Mama's goal.

I shared all of this hurt with the psychologist. In my sharing with him, I began to realize I had stuffed all of that anger and resentment for over twenty years. It was not just the treatment I had received but also what I saw white and Jewish people do to my parents. My parents were afraid to answer back because they had to feed all nine of us.

I later found out that the psychologist had studied for the priesthood. So, he knew the Bible. God had set me up. This man turned out to be a godsend. He listened to me long enough to ask the right questions—to get me to hear myself answer. He also was able to see how much I love the Lord—that in the center of who I am, is Jesus the Christ.

I had no idea how sick I was with unforgiveness. I also realized that because unforgiveness is sin, I had given place to the devil in my life. I could see it in my physical body.

On one occasion, I was visiting a friend. I bent down to pick up something and couldn't straighten back up. Another time, I reached to close my car door and something popped in my back. I couldn't straighten up or walk without excruciating pain for three weeks. I believe now it was only unforgiveness. I had been *handed over to the torturers* as it talks about in Matthew 18:34.

I heard a preacher say that unforgiveness is a poison you drink, hoping the other person/people will die. The reality is that it will kill **you**. It will kill you because it is sin and *the wages of sin is death but the gift of God is eternal life through Jesus Christ our Lord* (Romans 6:23).

THE JOURNEY TO FORGIVENESS

After I got through reliving the past and its pain, I went back to West Virginia. I revisited some of those places where I had been wronged. I forgave all of those people I had unknowingly held prisoners of my unforgiveness. They didn't have to be present because forgiveness had to happen in me. Forgiveness means to release it, let it drop, and let it go.

The crazy thing about all of this is that I knew I had to forgive. Remember, I know the Bible. I used to teach it, but I wasn't living it. Whether the people were dead or alive, when I forgave them by speaking it out loud, shackles fell from me. I was released from that prison and I also released them. Forgiving people is not a natural act. The Holy Spirit was the delivering force behind my actions.

In counseling, I talked about Ronnie and how he had made me feel ugly, useless, and such a hassle to him. I began to know and hear those lies for what they were: lies.

I went home and wrote on my bathroom mirror in bright red lipstick, "You are a wonderful person. You are a beautiful person. You are valuable and precious to God. God loves you with an everlasting love. You are the apple of your Father's eye. I love me. I am worth loving. You are a woman of worth. You are intelligent. You matter. God will never leave you or forsake you." I began to come to myself.

One important thing I found out about believing lies: Once you see they are lies, you have to come against them, full force, with the truth. I came at them with all the truth I knew. I was angry that I had cowered under Satan's **attempt** to kill me. It will not happen.

I began to hear myself say, "This is not the end of the world for me. I can do all things through Christ, which strengthens me. Lord, I know there is nothing too hard for You. Lord, You are my husband. I know You will take real good care of me. I'm mad <u>at</u> hell and I'm not going to take this any more."

After three months of weekly counseling, the counselor told me, "You are fine. You don't need to come to me any more. I would like to know if you would consider being a consultant for my practice?" I had to laugh, but I agreed to do so. God is so good.

A few months after ending my counseling, I began to receive negative credit inquiries about Ronnie and financial transactions he was making. Hence, I sought the counsel of an attorney. He advised me that as long as I was married to Ronnie Calloway, I was still liable for debts he might incur. Anything illegal he might do could come back on me.

I had to pay for some things that I wasn't expecting. I paid them because I could not let him destroy my credit. If my job sent me to Africa, which in fact it did, my credit card would have to work at hotel check-out. As much as I hated to, I got the divorce papers. Chaunci typed them for me.

THREE STRIKES...YOU'RE OUT

Three times, the divorce failed to go through. The Lord gave Ronnie three chances to go and contest it. He never did. The day the divorce was final, both of us met at the courthouse. Ronnie tried to faint at the clerk's counter. The clerk was LaVone, a friend of ours. She didn't want to have anything to do with the dissolution of our marriage because she cared about both of us.

LaVone asked, "Why don't you guys step outside in the hall and talk before you sign the papers?"

We got outside and Ronnie gently nudged me back against the wall and said, "Jack, why are you doing this? You know you love me."

"That is exactly why I'm doing this. You are still thinking about *you*. Why couldn't you say that you love me? No, let's get right back in here and sign these papers." We did that.

The atmosphere was surreal–like someone had died. I guess numb would best describe my feelings, like being in a vacuum.

I left the courthouse. When back at my job, my boss said to me, "I have something for you." She didn't know I had just gotten a divorce. She gave me a five-thousand dollar raise in pay that day.

God had told me to trust Him and stay in a giving place. I was obedient to Him and He was and is faithful to His Word. I never skipped a tithe or offering. And, I helped as many people as I could, including Ronnie.

After all of that, later that night Ronnie came over and we made love. Then, went our separate ways.

About a year after Ronnie and I divorced, I met a man who was eight years my junior. He swept me off my feet. He had a good job that he had worked for about twenty years. That was important to me. He was tall, handsome, loved music and hung on every word I said.

I could be in the middle of a sentence and he would interrupt me and say, "Do you know how beautiful you are?" I would melt. He called me every single day, long distance, and talked for hours. He played songs to me that told me how much he loved me. He sang to me. I thought I was in love. He wanted me to marry him right away.

HE'S STILL KICKING
One day I heard myself say, "This man is too good to be true." I told the Lord, "If there is anything I should know about him, show me." The very next time I was with him, I saw his temper. I found out he had the potential to be an abuser. Just as I said, he was too good to be true–but Jesus had my back.

Often, people who have been hurt or recently divorced, seek comfort and pain-relief from another broken and needy person. That never works. We look to that person to give us what the last person didn't. Sometimes you **can** get from that person what you didn't get from the last. Most of the time, though, you get something you didn't want…and didn't know you were getting. Ronnie did a lot of things, but he never once hit me or called me anything but Jackie. I thank God for that.

During my years of being single, I was able to clearly see the profile of an abuser. Usually, abusers come on very strong and are extremely nice…at first. Abusers often have taken the time to find out what makes you tick, what is important to you, and what turns you on. Skillfully, they learn your essence, your deficiencies, and your weakness.

In the beginning, they are very complimentary and flattering. But remember, one of the definitions of flattery is a dangerous, slippery place. At some point, they reveal a volatile side. At first, the fury may not be directed toward you. They are usually private people. Many of these personality types don't have close personal friends. They make you feel like you are so special to them that they want you all to themselves.

Over and over again, in different ways, they tell you "the type of person I am." They subtly begin to separate you from your friends and family by telling you little things they don't like about them.

At first, they are very romantic, hanging on your every word and making you feel you are the only important person in the world. They call you all the time. They give you nice gifts to bait you. They make you think they need you and no one else. The point being– and I repeat–when you open the door through sin, you can't always control what comes in. I have learned all of this from experience. As Mama used to say, "I've been around Jake's barn and got kicked by the mule. So, hear my wisdom and you don't have to go there." I found out that mule is still back there…and he is still kicking.

CHAPTER 10

WEDDING MADNESS

Chaunci informed me that she and her best friend, Clayton, wanted to get married. She said she believes he is the man God wants her to marry. Hearing that felt strange to me. Here I was, fighting to emotionally survive a divorce, and she wanted to get married.

I had no problem with her getting married to Clayton because I liked him. I could see that he loved her, very much. I just wanted to make sure she wasn't marrying out of hurt or trying to fill a void her father had caused. She assured me that was not the case.

We began to talk about her marriage. I couldn't resist telling Chaunci that if she knew what I knew about marriage, she should forget it and go play checkers. That was the Lillie Smith coming out in me. Mama could say some things that would make you go "Hummmmmm!"

Actually, helping Chaunci to plan her wedding was fun. For one reason, she wanted to do it right. They were both virgins and had not even kissed. He just followed her around like a little puppy.

I asked Ronnie to share Chaunci's wedding expenses and preparation and he agreed. We put all of the plans for the wedding on paper. I would pay for the church, the pastor, the clubhouse for the reception and any loose ends. Clay's grandmother bought the dress. Several months earlier, Ronnie's aunt, Sandy, had given Chaunci some money, which she put on her school bill. Yet, she was kind enough to pay for the wedding limousine as well. Ronnie would cater the food for the reception and purchase the cake—he is a great cook and caterer.

HE RENEGED!

Everything was going as planned until three days before the wedding. Ronnie showed up at my apartment, which happened to be on the third floor and said, "I am not going to do the reception. I don't have the money."

We were standing outside on the third floor balcony when he told me that. My first impulse was to push him over the banister and hope he landed on his head. I cannot tell you how angry I was.

Chaunci is his baby daughter. She had always worked hard and done well in school. There was never a rebellious bone in her body. She was very respectful and never gave us one minute of trouble in her life.

It was quite perplexing to me why Ronnie couldn't fix the food and buy the cake for the reception. I was livid. I could feel heat coming from the collar of my blouse. I could feel my ears burning. He disgusted me. I just turned and walked away.

After I had prayed and calmed down, Clayton's mother, Sondra and I went out to order a cake and meat and cheese trays at the grocery store. My good friend Ronnette, worked like a slave to help us pull this reception off. But *God doeth all things well*. It was a beautiful, wonderful wedding and reception.

They also had a great honeymoon in Florida. By the way, even though Ronnie did not cater the reception, he refused to be left out. Ronnie had ordered the limousine driver to pick him up so he could ride with Chaunci and her bridal party to the church. Can you stand it? Chaunci and Rhonda, her sister, were in shock.

Meanwhile, what did I learn from all the wedding madness? I was reminded that *Through Christ all things are possible*. No matter what

happens, God has everything in my life under control. I don't have to push anybody off of a third floor balcony or anything like that. I just have to crucify my flesh, pray and wait for the answer.

You may find yourself in some impossible place today, but don't panic. *Be still and know that He is God* (Psalm 46:10). If you just ask Him what to do, *He will direct your paths* (Proverbs 3:6). I'm a living witness.

CHAPTER 11

DISCOVERING WHO I WAS NOT

"Forgive me Lord but I'm still angry!" I was still angry and still drinking. I was offered a job in Augusta, Georgia and the Lord told me to take it. If you looked at it from a monetary standpoint, it didn't really make sense. I had to take a huge cut in pay and move myself from Colorado to Georgia. But, God told me to do it. He provided the finances for me to move there in July of nineteen ninety-five.

I absolutely loved Augusta but I didn't like my job. First of all, I wasn't really qualified to do the job. Secondly, it was different from what I had imagined. I soon came to realize, however, that it was a set up. God had set me up, again.

I knew only one person in Augusta, the person who hired me. Every night after work, I would go home to my apartment, and it would just be God and me. He had moved me out of my comfort zone, away from all of my props and the support of my children and friends. He had my undivided attention.

God began to talk to me and show me *my* part in the divorce. He showed me how self-righteous I had been. He showed me how I had beaten Ronnie over the head with the scriptures. I said, "Lord, don't you think he needed to beaten over the head with something?"

He showed me how I had usurped Ronnie's authority over and over again by not letting him be the man. If he said he wasn't going to pay something, I would find a way to pay it myself. I said, "Well Lord, did you want me to let the gas and lights go off?" He said, "If necessary, yes. If you hadn't always been so quick to take charge, Ronnie would have had to."

CAUGHT THOUGH NOT TAUGHT

I was dumbfounded. I thought about what God had said. I replayed different scenarios in my head. He was absolutely right. I had been trained well by a take charge mother. She had to be in charge. For years, my daddy, who was a coal miner, was only home on occasional weekends. I am certainly not blaming anything on my mother or father. But, I could clearly see how I had caught certain things that weren't intentionally taught.

How sobering it is to think that our children are being trained in our homes, every day. It might be the classes Selfishness 101, Pride 101, Anger 201, Fear 201, or Trusting God 301. We don't always realize that whatever we do and exhibit everyday, our children are watching. They are listening and absorbing our good and bad examples. At some point in their lives, they become us, as we have become our parents.

God said to me, "You were always more interested in church than you were in what Ronnie wanted to do." I replied, "Lord, all Ronnie ever wanted to do was play golf."

"Precisely. And, you wouldn't play with him."

"But Lord, that is just a game. I'm thinking about life, the kids, our future."

"Golf is an important part of <u>his</u> life. And, you refused to recognize that fact."

"Okay Lord, but what about the other women?" God said, "They played with him." That answer made me furious. I decided that was enough talk for the night. I poured myself a tall glass of champagne, drank it, and went to sleep.

These conversations went on night after night, and week after week. God showed me that my continued anger was a sure sign that I had not yet forgiven Ronnie. I said, "Lord, I have forgiven him; I am tired of hearing about him. I want to be free of him."

He said, "Who are you to hold you and Ronnie prisoner? How can you not forgive him, from your heart? You say you have forgiven him with your mouth, but your heart is still defiled. There is still so much poison there."

"Lord, how can there still be poison there?"

"Bitterness has taken root and it has to be cut out."

"Cut out?"

"Yes, with *the sword of the Spirit*, which is My Word. You took offense over and over again."

I pondered that fact and it was true. I was offended at God for not fixing Ronnie. I was offended at Ronnie for betraying me for so many years. I was offended at people who seemingly had happy marriages. I was offended at people who did not get a divorce. I was angry at myself for going back into the world and sin. I was an angry, depressed, addicted mess.

I had pretty much anesthetized myself with alcohol to the point at which I started to believe I was normal. I thought, "I'll be alright if I just continue to swim in denial–like so many people do." However, God refused me the luxury of drowning myself in that deceitful river.

God had slowly picked off the scabs of my emotions and they were bleeding and oozing pus. I told God exactly how I felt. I told Him how Ronnie had betrayed me and how He had let him betray me. I told Him how hurt and wounded I was from this whole ordeal. "My life is destroyed and devastated. I don't deserve this," I cried until I was dry. There were no more tears.

I had gotten it all out of me and laid it before the Lord; and, I was limp. It was so good to get it all out again. I recommend that therapy to anyone who is still hurt, bitter and angry. Write your own psalms like David did in the Bible. You can speak it to God or write it and then tear it up and throw it away. Then, you can see it for what it is, garbage.

ENOUGH IS ENOUGH

Finally, my thinking changed, "Okay Lord, I just want to be whole! I don't care if I never see Ronnie Calloway again. I don't care if I ever get married again. All I know right now is that there is a call on my life and I just want to be whole. I want to finally be able to lift my eyes, above the situation, and move forward in life. I am tired, defiled and disgusted with myself."

Extremely disappointed in myself, I felt like such a failure. You never could have told me I would become an alcoholic, never. Nonetheless, I will repeat, when you open the door to sin, you inadvertently let in the consequences as well. But now, I had had enough.

Once I surrendered my will, wholly, to my heavenly Father–and said it with my mouth–things began to change. He continued to surface things in my heart that were not pleasing to Him. As He did, I would say to Him, "Father I see that and I confess it as sin. I repent and ask you to forgive me. I put this sin under the blood of Jesus."

This time, I truly forgave Ronnie. I wrote down everything I wanted to tell him about how he had wounded and almost killed me. I wrote page after page. At the end of the letter I wrote, "But, I forgive you, in the name of Jesus, by the blood of the lamb." Hebrews 9:22 teaches that without the shedding of blood there is no remission of sin.

I had sinned by not forgiving Ronnie, from my heart, a long time ago. Now, I had to get it right. Then, I tore the letter up. However, I remembered the date I forgave him. I knew the devil would try to come back at me with old memories. When he did, I said out loud, "Father God, I thank You that I forgave Ronnie on that date in Jesus name."

"If we confess our sins, He is faithful and just to forgive our sins and to cleanse us from all unrighteousness." (1 John 1:9) I could feel the cleansing process begin. I became stronger, physically. I was drinking

less and less. I still would smoke a joint, when I could get one; but, that was not often.

Mentally, my head was trying to clear. I know some of you are probably saying, "God doesn't talk to drunks." I beg to differ. He has to talk to drunks and dope addicts or they would never get sober. You have to remember these are the class of people Jesus hung out with when He walked the earth, prostitutes and *winebibbers*.

Some of my friends would never have talked to me if they had known what I was doing. My Father God however, continued to talk to me and encourage me through this whole ordeal. Sometimes, He would just say to me, "I love you." That would always bring me to my knees. You know, *"the goodness of God leadeth* [men/women] *to repentance."* (Romans 2:4)

Approximately a week later, Ronnie called and asked if he could come to see me. I agreed. I thought that would be fun. I was very lonesome and oh so horny. I also wanted to see if I had really forgiven him, from my heart. I knew if I could look him in the face and maybe make love with him that I would know for sure.

We talked on the phone a few nights, prior to him coming; Hence, the suspense was great. When he arrived, I was more than excited. I was glad to see him. He looked so much better than he did when I last saw him. He had gained a little weight and was all smiles. We embraced and Ronnie held me real close. But, it was different. It wasn't the same. It felt real good, but it was not the same.

I invited him to make himself at home and showed him around my apartment. He was impressed with everything, especially my choice of furniture.

I took him out on the town and showed him a nice time. We ate well and we did a lot of talking. We had fun. He asked me to forgive him for all he had done to me. He told me how wrong he had been and asked me if I would take him back. He said, "I came down here to Augusta to throw my line in one more time."

I told him I had forgiven him before he came to town. As I looked in his eyes, I knew I truly had forgiven him and I honestly wished him all the best. "Ronnie I love you, but you are not in my future." I was very calm about it and very sincere.

"Are you sure?"

"Yes."

"Okay."

We knew it was sin, but we made love. The next day, he was on his way. I have to admit, I was a bit afraid to have intercourse with him. I knew he had been with many women. I certainly took a serious chance. I also knew he had **always** had other women and God had protected me all of these years. I had a supernatural confidence that He would continue. I surprised myself. I wasn't sad or angry or bitter. I was starting to feel like my old, confidant self again, Hallelujah.

CHAPTER 12

TIME TO GET UP AND GROW

ime had gone by quickly and I had begun to dream again. I started to think about what type of business I wanted to start or what field I wanted to go into. I thought about starting a multi-cultural tour company. I developed the plan and put it all on paper. I thought it was a great idea.

I was sitting at my desk one day and I thought to myself, "You know Jackie, this is a job." It dawned on me that it had been a long time since I had had a job. I was used to holding positions. I left a position where they were paying me well for my opinion. On this job, I didn't feel like my opinion was valued one bit.

"Lord, I can sit here and continue to do a job, or I can get up and continue to grow."

"Get up."

"What? Lord, I have moved all the way across country, by myself. Now, You are telling me to get up?" I knew it was the Lord talking to me. Therefore, I began to pray about getting up. The more I prayed, the stronger my faith became. I knew I was moving in God's timing.

The Lord had convinced me *"To trust Him with all my heart and lean not to my own understanding, in all my ways to acknowledge Him and He would direct my paths."* He had drilled that into my head.

"Trust Me with your **whole** heart and I will direct your paths." That is what He told me, over and over again. That word *paths* has an *s* on the end of it. I knew that meant every little thing I did, I could trust Him to show me what and how to do it. I was fully persuaded, no looking back. I have come to know that this is faith in its purest form: Just believing what God says and acting on it.

Two weeks later, I had everything planned. I would move to Atlanta and start my tour company—with the help of the Lord and a good looking football coach I had just met there. I knew we could make it work. My faith in God's willingness to keep me was as strong as it had ever been.

I wrote my letter of resignation and met with my boss. She asked me, "Do you have another job offer?"

"No."

"What are you going to do for money?"

"I will trust in the Lord with all of my heart and lean not to my own understanding, in all my ways I'll acknowledge Him and He will direct my paths." She looked at me like I had lost my mind; but, she accepted my resignation and I left three weeks later.

BORN AGAIN...AGAIN

When I left that job, I felt like I was living John 8:36 which says, *"If the Son therefore shall make you free, ye shall be free indeed."* No reflection on the job or any of the people, it was just time for me to leave. The Lord worked everything out for me. A sweet lady, who had befriended me on the job, bought all of my furniture. That was just God's way of *supplying all of my need according to His riches in glory by Christ Jesus.*

Have you ever felt like you had been born again, again? Has God ever given you another chance? I slowly realized I was forty-seven years young; I had my whole life before me. I had been put in position, by

God Almighty, to do and be all that He had designed me to be. There were no strings attached—just wisdom from Him.

I experienced a feeling of euphoria. I knew, without one doubt, God was going to take very good care of me. It was almost as if I was in a protective bubble. I knew that anybody or anything that tried to get to me had to go through Him first. According to Hebrews 4, I was living in God's divine rest. I did not have a care in the world. Even though I had no job and I was homeless, my *"life was hid with Christ in God"* (Colossians 3:3). That kind of assurance is called, *"That peace that passes understanding"* (Philippians 4:7).

There was this overwhelming sense of excitement and anticipation in my heart. I knew something good was about to happen to me because, *"Eye hath not seen, nor ear heard, neither have entered into the heart of man, the things which God hath prepared for them that love him"* (1 Corinthians 2:9).

After leaving Augusta, I went to Ronnie's sister's house in Marietta, Georgia. I put some of my things in her garage and spent the night. The next day, I had this overwhelming urge to see my children and grandchildren in Denver. I thought I would go there and spend a couple of weeks relaxing before returning to Atlanta to get an apartment and start my business. I knew Ronnie's sister, Donna, and her husband, Patterson, would let me stay with them until I got a place.

I prayed and asked the Lord if I could go to Denver to see my children. He said, "Yes". I was so excited. Knowing I would only be gone for a short time, I packed only the clothes I thought I would need for approximately a week; then, I drove to Denver.

It was a wonderful trip. I took all of my music and teaching tapes with me. I sang, prayed, and praised the Lord all the way. It was a two-day drive. I stopped in Columbia, Missouri, got a hotel, spent the night, and continued on the next day. I arrived in Denver late that afternoon.

I went straight to Rhonda's apartment to see her and my little grandson, Azlan. I had missed them all so much. When I got there, Rhonda said, "Mom, Dad is looking for you. He wants you to call him."

"Call him for what?"

"I don't know, but he wants to see you."

Immediately, the phone rang and it was Ronnie. He was so glad to talk to me. He said, "I knew you had no business in Augusta. I knew that job wasn't going to work out. I'm glad you're back. I am going to go out of town this weekend and you can stay here at my apartment, if you would like. You don't have to stay over there with those babies crying. You are welcome to stay here."

"Thank you, but I came here to see these crying babies. I will be fine."

"At least you could come over and just see the apartment. You can stay if you want to; if not, that's fine." I said, "Okay, maybe I will come later."

I spent time with Rhonda and cute little Azlan. He has the greatest blue eyes and a big head like Ronnie. Then, I went to Chaunci's house where I intended to sleep. They had made room for me, and I was so glad to see those pretty little babies. It was so good to hold them and kiss them and to let them kiss me. Jacqueline Michelle is my namesake. I was so honored when Clay and Chaunci named her after me. The ironic thing is that she looks just like me. She has the prettiest dark brown eyes, curly black hair, and perfectly formed, cover girl lips. She is beautiful. Then there is Joshua. He was just a few months old and looks like Ronnie. I had missed my family more than I imagined. It felt so good to see and touch them all again.

Ronnie called again, very late that night. He said, "I will leave my key under the mat for you just in case you decide to come. I am leaving now for the weekend and I want you to know that you always have a home with me."

"Okay, I'll go over there before the night is over." I wasn't thinking about Ronnie Calloway. I wasn't mad at him because I was completely healed from all the hurt he had caused me. My mind was clear. I was so glad to see my children. For the first time, in months, I was genuinely happy. I didn't want anything or anybody to disturb my peace.

THIS IS A TEST–THIS IS ONLY A TEST

Finally, after the grandbabies were asleep, I was tired. I told the kids I was going to go to their dad's apartment and get some sleep. I wasn't excited about going to his apartment because I didn't really know what to expect. I knew once I had told Ronnie he was not in my future that he wouldn't waste any time securing female companionship. I knew he had to have at least two other women, right then. After twenty eight plus years, you get to know a person.

Arriving at the apartment, I opened the door. Oh my goodness, the place was beautiful. He had everything perfectly arranged. He had all white furniture and turquoise accessories. He had our old mirrors, a waterbed and nice pictures. Everything was spotless, smelling oh so fresh and clean.

He also had everything I liked in the refrigerator. He had shrimp, grapes and anything else he thought I would like. All I had to do was come in and put my feet up. Ronnie had made it very comfortable for me. I slept well that night.

The next day, the phone rang over and over and over again. I started not to answer but I did. "Hello. No, Ronnie is not here." There were different women calling for him day and night. What amazed me was they didn't care that another woman was answering his phone. They just left message after message. A couple of them asked who I was and I told them Jackie Calloway, to which each one replied, "Ronnie's daughter?"

"No," and they proceeded to leave a message anyhow. I thought, "Wow! Women are tough and bold out here." After a while, I became agitated when I thought about Ronnie asking me to stay here knowing all those women would be calling. Meanwhile, I began to snoop around the apartment. I found a sexy card from one chick, thanking him for dinner the other night and hoping he enjoyed what she gave to him. Nothing had changed. But what was I getting upset about? Ronnie was not my husband. We had been legally divorced for seven years. I had a whole new life now and a handsome fellow whom I had just met, waiting for me back in Atlanta. I had to just calm down. This was a test; this was only a test.

Once I got my thinking straight, I had a very nice day. I rested and tried to eat everything I could in that refrigerator. I went to see my children again and was so relaxed and happy I could hardly stand it.

That night, I returned to Ronnie's apartment and slept soundly. I had just gotten out of bed on Sunday morning when Ronnie came through the door. This huge smile crossed his face as he came in the kitchen, wrapped me in his arms so tightly and began to kiss me like he was Romeo or somebody. He held me back from him and looked at me from head to toe. He smiled again and said, "You look so good. I'm so glad you are here."

"I'm glad I'm here too and it's good to see you also." He acted as if he didn't want to let me go.

"Have you had breakfast? Can I fix you breakfast?"

"Sure."

"Yes, let me fix you some pancakes and eggs."

Ronnie has always been an excellent cook; as a matter of fact, he taught me how to cook. But even though this scene was familiar, it still seemed awkward. I guess I felt as though I had to keep my guard up so there wouldn't be any possibility of me getting hurt again.

We had a great breakfast. We laughed and talked small talk.

"How was your weekend? Where did you go?"

"I went on a golf trip with the fellows."

I didn't believe a word he said. We talked about the grandbabies and how cute and sweet they are. He comments how much little Jacqui looks like me and Josh and Azlan look like him. It was all very pleasant and superficial.

"Jack, you know I still love you. We ought to be together. Why don't you stay here with me?"

"Ronnie, I love you too but I'm not going to put myself back in the position to be crushed again. Besides, you have a ton of messages from a group of women. They have been calling here, night and day, since you left. So, don't tell me you love me. I don't want to hear that."

Right then, the phone rang and it was another woman. I honestly wasn't upset with him; but, I didn't want to be there any longer. I started getting my clothes together to go to Chaunci's house. I could hear Ronnie in the background trying to hurry the woman off of the phone. He got off the phone and said, "Jack, none of these calls are important to me because I love you."

I said, "Yea right. Well, right now my mind is on my future and what I'm going to do next. I left and went to Chaunci and Clay's house.

JUST TRUST ME

Before I left Augusta, I had been doing some consulting work with the General Board of Global Ministries in New York City. They had asked me to attend a training session in Oakland, California. I agreed to do so. This would be a three or four day trip. I left Denver and flew to Oakland.

The staff stayed in a very nice hotel, as usual. I remember standing in front of the window in my room with a perfect view of the Bay Bridge. I was thinking, "This is so beautiful." Just then, the Spirit of the Lord said to me, "I want you to start listening to Ronnie Calloway."

I screamed at the top of my voice, "NO! NO! I won't listen to him. You know he's a liar. You know I can't trust him!" That same voice said to me so gently, "I'm not asking you to trust him right now. I'm asking you to *Trust Me with all your heart and lean not to your own understanding, in all your ways acknowledge Me and I will direct your paths.*"

I was furious. I could not believe God was asking me to put myself in that vulnerable position again. I felt like all of my hopes and plans for the future were instantly dashed like a champagne glass thrown against a fireplace. I stomped my foot and yelled,

"That's not fair God. That's not fair. How can you let him just walk back into my life after all he has done to me? God this is not fair. All of those times, God, he lied to me. He has cheated on me. You know he has had intercourse with other women, probably even some that I thought were my friends. I can't believe You are going to just let him have his way with me again. God, that is not right. I will not do this. I will not let Ronnie Calloway ruin my life again. God I don't understand. You told me to trust You and now You are telling me this. It's not right, God, not after it has taken me all of these years to heal. God no, no, no I can't do it. God don't you remember I wanted to die? I wanted to commit suicide and You walked me through that. Don't You remember how depressed I was for so long? God, don't you remember how I couldn't get my head off the pillow? Oh God, no. Don't do this to me. I can't take the pain. No, I won't listen to Ronnie again ever."

I was crying uncontrollably. As I write these words, reliving the horrible shock and fear of losing everything…again… I am crying–even now. I dread being made a fool of, seeing the prideful gloat on Ronnie's face, just the humiliation of it all. This is so unfair.

"God, when is it my turn to have the very best? When do I get rewarded for some of the good things I've done in life? When is my number chosen? I always have to sacrifice for somebody else. It is always Jackie behind the eight ball. Well, I won't listen to Ronnie. I will not do it. I can't stand to be hurt one more time. Find somebody else to kill."

All the while I was fussing at God, I knew I was going to do whatever He told me to do. I had surrendered my will to Him in Augusta. And, no matter how I ranted and raved and no matter how long it took, I knew, deep in my heart, that I would eventually obey my Father. And, He knew it too. I could see He had set me up again.

It took me three days to get myself together. I went out and bought myself a bottle of champagne. I drank and I cried. I drank and I slept. When I would wake up, I'd just lie there. I was just still and quiet. Every once in a while, I would say, "No, no, this is not fair." Then, on the third day, I began to pray. I don't know yet what that training meeting was about. I honestly cannot tell you.

I prayed and asked God, "Why are you doing this to me? Why Lord?" Then I remembered what He said to me, years earlier, when I asked Him why. "The question is not why but what now? Are you going to obey Me?" I took several deep breaths and I said nothing. I couldn't bring myself to answer.

When I look back on those three days, it was the death and burial and of my flesh and my will. It came down to, "Not my will, Lord, but Yours be done." How merciful God is to us. There are some who will cringe, reading how I yelled at God. I cringe myself, sometimes, when I think about it. But, 1 Chronicles 16:34 says, "*His mercy endureth for ever.*" I am learning what that means. He extends to us all the mercy we need to get us to where He wants us to be.

The other factor is He knows our hearts. Jeremiah 17:10 says, "*I the* LORD *search the heart, I try the reins, even to give every man according to his ways, and according to the fruit of his doings.*"

WHAT ABOUT *MY* LIFE?

When I got on that plane, going back to Denver from Oakland, I was so weak that I didn't know what to do. I was feeling like a rung out dishrag. But, I had made the quality decision to obey the Lord. I still hadn't told Him yet, even though He knew.

I kept thinking about all those women calling Ronnie's apartment. "What is he going to do with them? Ronnie probably doesn't really want me anyway. He's probably saying he loves me just to make conversation. Anyway, if he did want me why was he dating all those women? I know he's a single man, but none of this makes sense to me."

I kept thinking about my plans. "What about my multi-cultural tour company? What about living in Atlanta? What about **my** life?" I didn't say anything. I was just thinking about it all. I was breathing but I was numb.

CHAPTER 13

WHOSE LIFE IS IT ANYWAY?

After returning to Denver, my children convinced me to stay there with them until after Christmas. That sounded good to me because I was feeling real shaky at that point. I needed some affirmation. I needed to be with my children. I know they love me very much.

The very next day, I slept in late. I had thought myself into exhaustion. I was awakened by the telephone. Of course, it was Ronnie. He said, "Good morning," with his deep sexy voice. "Good morning," I replied. He said, "Please let me take you to lunch today." I agreed and he was there in less than an hour.

Although it was November, it was still a bright, sunny day in Colorado. We laughed and talked and remembered some good old times. We had a great afternoon.

While driving back to Chaunci's house, I said to him, "You know Ronnie, maybe, possibly, there might be some way, if you really want to, that we could see if you would be able to, maybe try to rebuild the trust between me and you."

I was not trying to be definite at all. I really didn't want to ask him if he wanted to do anything. But, I was compelled by the Christ in me to obey God, my Father.

Ronnie was shocked. He was so shocked that he hesitated a long time as if he was thinking, "Are you sure? Why are you saying this now? I don't know what to say." I immediately took offense and said, "Now you certainly don't have to if you don't want to. You're the one who told me you loved me and said we ought to be together, not me."

He quickly said, "No, no, I'm just surprised you're saying this. You said I was not in your future. Why are you saying this now?"

I mumbled, "Because God told me to listen to you. He didn't tell me to marry you. He just told me to listen to you. Therefore, I know if I'm going to listen to you at all, I have to be able to trust you. So, do you want to do this or not?"

"Yes, yes by all means," he answered. "I asked the Lord to send you back to me and I do want to do this."

"Ronnie you know trust is earned and I don't trust you at all and you know why."

"Yes I know; but I'm going to do everything I can to build trust between us."

"I'm not promising you anything, Ronnie. As a matter of fact, I have a lot of questions I never got answered that I want to talk about."

"Jack just give me a chance to rebuild the trust."

"Ha," I thought to myself, "You'll be a good one if you do, buddy." But again, I didn't say anything out loud.

It was an adventure talking to each other and seeing who we had become. I was forty-seven and he was fifty-one. We had four grandchildren. I kept thinking, "I'm listening to this old rascal again. I might want a young man from here on out. Why not, Jack? He's always wanted a young woman." But, I didn't say anything out loud.

The next day, we were at his apartment. I questioned him about many things that had happened since we were divorced. I asked, "What happened that turned you around and caused you to stop smoking dope?"

"Jack, do you remember how you used to pray and ask God to speak to me face to face, just like He did Moses?"

"Yes."

"I had lived in a van for four months. The van didn't even run. Well, God met me nose to nose, one Sunday morning. I stepped out of that van and God said to me, 'You can't live without Me.' I stepped back into that van, put on a suit, and caught the bus to church. I repented and asked God to forgive me for all the wrong I had done. Later, I asked Him to send my family back to me. Even though I asked God to do that, I didn't think there was any chance of it ever happening. Therefore, I continued to look for a Christian woman. I dated many women—some Christians and some not."

My first thought was, "Tell me something I **don't** know. I read that chick's thank you card last week. I know she wasn't saved."

"By the way," I said, "if you are going to try to build trust with me, what are you going to do with those women, who are calling here all the time?" He said, "You just give me twenty-four hours and I'll take care of them."

I want you to know that in twenty-four hours, all of those women stopped calling, all except one. She was determined. But, I know how Ronnie was and I'm sure he had made her think they would be together forever.

He told me that I could answer his phone whenever I was there. When I would, this woman would hang up on me. That made me so angry. I asked Ronnie, "Do we need to go to her house and talk to her?"

"No you don't need to do anything. I will handle this tonight." So he went to her house. I know he probably slept with her once more. I don't know. I only knew I didn't trust Ronnie as far as I could throw him. I said, "If you want this woman, you can have her. I will go on back to my life." He had the nerve to tell me he *did* like her but he really loved me and he wanted us to stay on track.

I must confess to you that I still wanted to beat Ronnie in the face with my high heel shoe, from time to time, but I couldn't. For once, in all the years I had known him, he was doing everything right.

THE INQUISITION

I would ask him very personal questions like "When you were screwing so-and-so, where did you go to do it?" I tried to be as crass and abrasive as I could. He would say, "We went to such-a-such hotel. I was wrong. please forgive me."

Next I asked, "When I asked you if you were doing it to so and so and you told me no, were you lying?"

"Yes, Jack, I'm so sorry. Please forgive me."

"How long have you cheated on me?"

"I always thought I should have another woman."

"How could you have done that to me Ronnie? All I ever wanted to be was Mrs. Ronnie Calloway. How could you have dogged me like that?"

He said without touching me, "Jack, please, please forgive me. I **love** you and I was not in my right mind. All the time I was smoking marijuana, I had this delusional opinion of myself. I realize how much I have hurt you. All I want you to do is give me the chance to make it up to you. I love you with all my heart."

"Ronnie you can't begin to fathom how much you hurt me. You betrayed the girls and me. You lied to me, looking me in the face, and tried to make me think I was crazy. You have no idea the damage you've done. So, don't even say that you know. Furthermore, I don't want to talk to you any more today."

"Jack, remember I love you." I walked quickly to my car without responding.

"God, this is impossible. This is too painful." As I drove home, I reflected on the entire conversation and realized that he was at least being truthful with me, I think. He was remorseful. If he had said "I'm sorry" one more time I would have puked. Could he really be sorry? If he is sorry, why does he want me back? All of those women he has screwed are younger, cuter, and less angry with him than I am.

Maybe he wants me back so he can get even with me for not taking him in when he was homeless, living in that van. Maybe he just wants to take advantage of me again. But, I don't have anything for him to **have** now. I don't have a job or house or anything. As a matter of fact, **I'm** homeless, and he has been spending **his** money on me.

As I thought more about it, I realized that I would get angry when I heard some of those answers he gave me, but I couldn't stay angry for long. I truly had forgiven him. The poison was gone. I had never heard some of these facts he was telling before, so processing them was brutally painful.

The next day, Ronnie called me with something funny to say to soften me up. Then, we got together and talked some more. I literally grilled him for information. These were questions I had thought about for years. Ronnie had lied so much in the past, I wanted to know all the truth. Surprisingly, he was forthright and told me what I wanted to know without getting angry with me.

One day, I said to him, "How do I know you are telling me the truth?" He said, "I am through telling lies. From now on, it's the truth and nothing but the truth." I found out later that statement was a lie, but it did get better as time went on.

I interrogated him for about three months—until I was tired of hearing the answers. I would get so emotional and cry when I found out the truth. I remembered how, at one time, he had me thinking I was crazy. He would often put his arms around me and try to comfort me.

THEN AND NOW

Some of the things Ronnie did when we were married were so foul. Back in those days, when I questioned him, he told me he was tired of being accused of something he wasn't doing. **Now** he has told me he was doing all those things I suspected, and more.

That was mental and emotional abuse. Recognize it ladies, especially if you are saved and filled with the Holy Spirit. Trust **your** spirit. The Holy Spirit reveals things to you sometimes that you are not even thinking about. I remember how deep in denial I was in the marriage. I saw many things that I really didn't want to see; but, didn't press the issues. Failing to do so made me physically sick and confused. I allowed our relationship to become toxic. I believed the lies and accepted the criticism that he heaped on me.

That was then and this is now. I was determined to be aware of and acknowledge every little thing I thought was suspicious. After all, I had nothing to loose.

Ronnie developed a method of measurement for keeping his word. He would tell me he was going somewhere and would be back in twenty minutes. But, he consistently returned in fifteen minutes. There was never a place I couldn't go with him. He was open with absolutely nothing to hide.

He said to me, "I'd like to take you to dinner tomorrow, if the Lord wills."

I thought, I've never heard him say that before. But, I have seen **temporary** conversions **before**. I was very impressed with how Ronnie was so prayerful about everything. He wasn't doing his own thing anymore; I could see he was being led by the Spirit of God.

Ronnie began to woo me as I began to trust him. He took me to dinner, lunch, movies, church, and to the park to feed the ducks. He frequently told me how much he loved me; and, he always made me laugh. He would remind me of some of the good old times we had. He would say things like "I didn't know how good I had it until I lost you. Jack, you have always been so good to me. I apologize again for hurting you." That would just melt me down.

ARE YOU SURE?

I told Chaunci and Clayton, "I'm considering getting back with your dad." They both panicked. Clayton, who talks very fast said, "Uh, Ms. Calloway, uh, I think you should give that some long and careful thought."

Chaunci said, "I know you have got to be kidding. What in the world are you considering that for? Have you forgotten all that you went through, Mom? All of that crying and pain and hurt he caused you? Just tell me why you are considering that?" She was visibly upset. I said, "Well, the Lord told me to listen to him."

"Yea, listen to Him, but don't marry him," she said. Clayton said, "Uh, yes, I totally agree with Chaunci. You know we love you and we don't want to see you hurt again."

"We love you and we don't want to see you get hurt again." That was the first of at least one hundred times I would hear **that** statement.

When I told Rhonda, she said, "Are you sure that's what you want to do?" She is her daddy's girl and had stayed in touch with him during our years of divorce. She tried to support him when she could. Therefore, I wasn't surprised at her response. But, I had no idea the opposition I would face from others.

You must understand. The thing about our divorce is that almost everybody knew about it. I didn't spare anyone the gory details when we broke up. Any one who would give me a shoulder, I cried on it. Our friends knew how hurt I was. They also saw Ronnie at the nightclubs with different women, old and young. Some even knew when he was homeless. I guess you could say folk knew our business.

A couple of my brothers thought I was crazy. But when I told my mother, Alzheimer's or not, she told me, "If it is at all possible for you to get back with Ronnie it would be a good thing. At least you know him. You wouldn't have to try to learn somebody new and then be disappointed when you find out who **they really** are."

When I told Ronnie about the children's reactions, he took them out to dinner. During the evening, he confessed to them that he had been unfaithful to me. He apologized to them and asked them to forgive him. To my astonishment, without hesitation, they did.

I asked Chaunci, "Did you forgive him that quick?" She said, "Yes, all I wanted to hear was the truth."

That amazed me because she had been so angry with her dad for the way he had treated us. I'll give you an example of why I was so surprised. Once, after Ronnie and I had separated, I lost my wedding ring. I couldn't find it anywhere. Chaunci asked, "Mom, when was the last time you've seen Dad?" I couldn't believe she was implying that

Ronnie might have taken my ring. I said to her, "You should be ashamed of yourself, Chaunci. That is your father."

"That's why I'm asking, because he is my father, and I know how he thinks. So, I repeat, when was the last time you've seen him?" I had never thought about it but he had been at my apartment the night before I missed the ring. To make a long story short, after a few weeks he brought the ring back to me. He said the last time he was at my apartment it fell into his bag. I was appalled.

For Chaunci to forgive him as easily as she did surprised me. But, at this point, I had to begin to recognize the move of God. If you have one eye, you can begin to see that God was in charge here. I remained prayerful, while continuing to try to catch Ronnie in **any** of his old ways. The Lord kept telling me to trust **Him** with all my heart; and, I did.

CHAPTER 14

ENGAGED TO GOD'S MAN

To my delight, things got progressively better. In February 1996, Ronnie got down on one knee and asked me to marry him. I said, "Yes." I could not believe I had come to this place. Over the months, he had thoroughly convinced me that he wanted me to be his wife again. We had not set a date yet but we both agreed that we should have pre-marital counseling. Our friend, Dr. Prescilla Lindsey, agreed to counsel us. She helped us wrap up some unfinished business.

Ronnie became skilled at wooing me. The closer we got, the more there were times when we would get a little steamy. But, I told him I wasn't going to have intercourse with him. He told me he didn't want me to because he wanted to make this marriage right, in the sight of God. He said we are definitely abstaining from sex until our wedding night. I was shocked to hear him say that. In the past, sex had been what he thought was his secret weapon on me. He said this time he was going to do this thing right and he did.

There was just one problem. **I was still drinking**. It wasn't as much as had been in the past, but I was still drinking. Ronnie began to ask me, "Don't you think you've had enough?" That would make me angry. I guess the more I trusted Ronnie, the more frightened I got. In the past, trusting him had always led to grave disappointment and hurt for me.

I was also feeling that I was doing fine on my own. I was enjoying my freedom to do what I wanted without any criticism from him or anyone else. He had done just what he wanted to do all of these years, at my expense. Now, he's going to do it again and I'm letting it happen.

I did have sense enough to know that I needed to be delivered from the alcohol. But, the more Ronnie complained about it, the more I drank. I couldn't believe he had stopped smoking dope. Maybe he'd have a drink every once in a while, but certainly nothing like me. If I bought a bottle of champagne, he might have one glass. I would drink the rest of the bottle.

DELIVERANCE

One day, I was by myself. I could see clearly what God was about to do. He was about to create a new marriage–a **God kind** of marriage. Marriage the way He originally designed it to be, in the beginning. He was giving us another chance to be happy. He was also giving **Ronnie** another chance. So, I went to the store, got a bottle of champagne and got drunk.

Only this time, I felt so guilty. I was so convicted that I cried out to God, "Lord, I know what You want to do and I want You to do it. I know too that if I don't get delivered, I'm going to mess this whole thing up. Father, this is the kind of marriage I have prayed for over twenty eight years; and now, I'm about to blow it. I remember Lord how on fire for You I was at one time. I remember how happy and dependent on You I was, Lord, without the dope and alcohol, but I don't know how to get back there Lord.

I prayed, *"Have mercy upon me, O God, according to thy lovingkindness: according unto the multitude of thy tender mercies blot out my trans-*

gressions. Wash me throughly from mine iniquity, and cleanse me from my sin. For I acknowledge my transgressions: and my sin is ever before me. Against thee, thee only, have I sinned, and done this evil in thy sight: that thou mightest be justified when thou speakest, and be clear when thou judgest. Behold, I was shapen in iniquity; and in sin did my mother conceive me. Behold, thou desirest truth in the inward parts: and in the hidden part thou shalt make me to know wisdom. Purge me with hyssop, and I shall be clean: wash me, and I shall be whiter than snow. Make me to hear joy and gladness; that the bones which thou hast broken may rejoice. Hide thy face from my sins, and blot out all mine iniquities. Create in me a clean heart, O God; and renew a right spirit within me. Cast me not away from thy presence; and take not thy holy spirit from me. Restore unto me the joy of thy salvation; and uphold me with thy free spirit. Then will I teach transgressors thy ways; and sinners shall be converted unto thee. Deliver me from bloodguiltiness, O God, thou God of my salvation: and my tongue shall sing aloud of thy righteousness." (Psalm 51:1-14)

I was literally crying tears of great sorrow and repentance. Those scriptures flooded my soul and burst forth out of my lips. I meant every word I cried. Then I lay down and cried myself to sleep with Psalm 51 going over and over in my head.

Psalm 119:11 says, *"Thy word have I hid in my heart, that I might not sin against Thee."* I know what that means now. Over the course of my life, I have studied the Word. I have had such a reverence and respect for the Word of God. Early in my childhood, I saw the principles of the Word lived out, through my mother. As I got older, I just listened to the preachers preach. They thought they knew what they were talking about. Some of them did, and some of them didn't. Later, as I shared in an earlier chapter, I became a student of the scriptures. Not so much memorizing but meditating on the Word.

Though I had sunk so far down in the horrible pit of sin, that Word I had put in my heart over the years, was strong enough to deliver me instantly from the alcohol addiction. From that day to this, I am delivered. Hallelujah!

CHAPTER 15

GOD CONDUCTS THE WEDDING

In March 1996, Ronnie came to me again, got down on one knee, took my hand and said, "Jackie Smith Calloway, I love you with all my heart. I know I have hurt you in the past; but, I want to make all of that up to you. You never have to work another day in your life, if you don't want to. I want to spend the rest of my life taking care of you and making you happy. Will you marry me?" He put a beautiful, three- karat, diamond ring on my finger and I said, "Yes, I will marry you."

We made the quality decision that from that day on, we would not go back and dig up the hurtful things of the past. We agreed we would live today and look to the future.

It is important that I explain to you how God performed miracles in our life. Take, for instance, my deliverance from alcohol. I have had no withdrawals, no AA, no desire to drink again. I am not a recovering alcoholic. I am delivered by the power and grace of God.

Next, Ronnie had only been on his job for a short time. When I came back to Denver, he was only making eight dollars and seventy-five cents an hour. That was certainly not enough for him to take care of me and make me happy for the rest of my life. Even the ring was a miracle.

Ronnie had bought a diamond ring for himself years ago. He had pawned it off and on during his time of homelessness. When he took that ring to see what he could trade it in for, it was worth enough to buy two wedding rings, one for me and one for him. **Amazing**.

Then, there was the wedding. I had thought we would just invite our children, a few friends, go to the church and have Dr. Lindsey marry us. But God had another plan. We certainly didn't have enough money for a wedding, but God's favor is better than money. As word got out that we were getting married, we got mixed responses. There were people who told us, individually, "You must be crazy." But then, there were others who were excited and expressed, "This is wonderful."

People called me saying, "I know you haven't invited me to the wedding, but I'm coming anyway." One of Ronnie's high school class-mates said, "I'm sending you a list of all the gang and their addresses. We'll see you at the wedding." I thought, "Lord, what are we going to do?"

He said, "Trust Me." I asked Ronnie, "How are we going to do this? He said, "I don't know but I sure do want to have all my friends there." I just began to pray. I didn't even have money for invitations or stamps. I took one step of faith at a time.

I went to the Curtis Park Community Center where our good friend, Jess Willis, was the director. I asked him if I could make some invitations on one of their computers. He said, "Of course." When I told him we were going to marry again, he was sincerely happy for us. I told him, "I don't know where we'll have the reception." He said, "You are welcome to have it here." I asked, "How much will that cost?" He said, "We'll work something out." He charged us forty dollars.

The Holy Spirit gave me the design for the invitation. On the front it said, *"Therefore if any person is (engrafted) in Christ (the Messiah) he is a new creation (a new creature altogether); the old (previous moral and*

spiritual condition) has passed away. Behold the fresh and new has come!"
(2 Corinthians 5:17 AMP)

Truer words have never been spoken. This marriage is new. I made copies of the invitations and was ready to hand deliver them. But wait, God had another plan.

Ronnie had asked his best friend, Dennis Irvin, to be his best man. He was honored to do so. Dennis said he didn't pay any attention to that divorce anyway. Then he told Ronnie he wanted to give him our gift early. He gave him two hundred dollars, cash. There was our stamp money for the invitations and more. We're talkin' El Shaddai here, the God Who is more than enough. I finally figured out that God was orchestrating this wedding. I began to relax and let Him do it.

I WANT THAT PART

Five days before the wedding, I was alone in Ronnie's apartment, sitting at the kitchen table. The Lord said to me, "You raised your hands at church yesterday and sang I surrender all." He continued, "You haven't surrendered all." I was stunned. I said, "Lord what else do You want from me?"

He said, "There is still a little part of your heart I want. When you divorced, you said, "I'll never let anybody get that close to me again. I'll never love anybody like I loved Ronnie again in my life." I certainly did remember saying that. God said, "I want that little part of your heart."

I had learned, by now, to obey quickly. I raised my hands and said out loud, "Lord, I surrender that part to you." That vow was so spiritually deep that it affected me physically. I felt the power of God come over me. My knees buckled. I thought I would fall to the floor, so I went quickly in and lay on the bed.

When the supernatural confronts the natural, the natural cannot stand. As I lay there, the Lord began to bring before me all of His goodness. It was almost like a slide show. It was an open vision. God took me back to my childhood, showing me the people He had put in my life to point me to Him.

My mother was the first face to appear. He said, "It isn't a coincidence that she is your mother. When you were born, she gave you back to me, and I took you." After each face He brought to me He said, "It was Me loving you through them." He showed me my childhood pastor, who really trained me in the things of God. He said, "It was Me loving you through him."

He brought me all the way up through the divorce. He showed me how He had protected me from evident danger while I was in sin. He reminded me of how He had supplied all of my needs, gave me raises, cars and filled my pockets with money when I could have been in poverty.

He said to me, "Now, I'm giving you a new marriage and a new husband and it will **always** be **Me** loving you, **through** him!"

He did open heart surgery on me that day. My Father, God, took out a stony heart and replaced it with a heart of flesh, which is pliable to Him and His will for me. He also put an uncommon love in my heart for Ronnie; a love that I had never known before. It is called agape, the God kind of love. All the past was blotted out. I love him, sincerely. I love him so deeply that I cry when I think about him and all God has done. It is *joy unspeakable and full of glory* (1 Peter 1:8). I got up a changed and grateful person.

CHAPTER 16

WOW, WHAT A WEDDING!

From nineteen eighty-six to nineteen ninety-five, I worked for the United Methodist Church Headquarters. Therefore, I went to the pastor at Scott United Methodist Church and asked what it would cost for us to be married there? He said no charge. Dr. Lindsey, who performed the ceremony, didn't charge us either.

Ronnie told me he had a little money saved and I could probably spend about one hundred and fifty to two hundred dollars on a dress. I was surprised because that was a lot of money for us at that time.

I said, "Okay, but I'm just going to look for a suit. I'm not looking for a real wedding dress." I searched for a dress in every department store I could find. One day, I was driving and the Holy Spirit said, "Why don't you go to the bridal shop?" I thought, "Dah, I think I'll go to the bridal shop; they have plenty of mother in-law dresses and suits there. I want something straight and plain not fancy, maybe in off white or cream."

As I stepped inside the bridal shop, the sales associate said, "May I help you?" I said, "Yes, I'm looking for your bargains." She said, "All of our sale dresses are on the wall with the red tags."

I said, "Thank you." I began to look. All of those dresses were four, five and six hundred dollars, marked down–all except one. This one had been marked down from six hundred dollars to one hundred and ninety-nine dollars and ninety-nine cents. I took it down off the rack and went to the dressing room to try it on. After looking at it closely, I found it to be a beautiful dress.

It was a **real** wedding dress. It was white, straight and floor length. It was off the shoulders with a deep satin collar that attached on the side. There were three, big, white, satin roses that went across the waist in the back. The roses attached a six-foot train. The amazing thing about this dress was that it fit me to a 'T'. I tried that dress on because it was the only size seven on the rack. This dress fit as though it had been custom made for me.

As I stood there admiring myself in front of the mirror the Holy Spirit said to me, "You can have that dress." I busted out laughing, "Yea, and people will think I have lost my mind. I have been married for twenty-eight years with three children and four grandchildren and I come down the aisle like I'm a virgin." But, I thought, "I am a virgin in God's eyes; because of the blood of Jesus He has made all things new again." God agreed, "Who cares what people think?" I said, "Lord, this is too much."

THE GIFT OF FAITH

He said to me again, but with a stern tone, "You can have that dress." This time, He imparted to me the *gift* of faith. You know there is the *act* of faith, when **you** believe for something. Then, there is the *gift* of faith, when God wants you to have it, whether **you** believe it or not. This was the *gift* of faith He put in me.

I took the dress off, walked out of the dressing room and the sales associate said, "Do you like that dress?" I said, "Yes I do, but you need to mark this down some more." Believe me, I had not thought about saying that. She said, "Why?" I said, "Because I might buy it if you do."

She paused, looked at me strangely and said, "Okay, how about forty-nine dollars and ninety-nine cents?" I almost fell to my knees.

I said, "I'll take it." I wrote that check so fast before she realized what she had done. I was in shock. The dress cost me forty-nine dollars and ninety-nine cents. My Father is more than enough.

I got in my car and I screamed, "Thank You Jesus. Hallelujah. Praise You Father. Lord, You are doing all of this and I thank You. Thank You. Thank You."

I have never been so excited in all of my life. I rushed home to show Chaunci. She said, "Oh, that's nice."

"Wow, that's great," I said. "Do you understand what I'm telling you? This dress cost me forty-nine ninety-nine." She said, "That's great Mom." Her reaction was somber. She was still cautiously concerned about my marrying her dad.

When I told Ronnie I only spent forty-nine ninety-nine on the dress, he said, "I'm sure it's nice." He told me later, he thought, "What in the world kind of dress has that girl bought?" He just could not imagine what it would look like. "I hope she won't look shaky coming down the aisle."

After that miracle, I got busy and planned a beautiful wedding. Now, our wonderful day is here. Once again, I can hardly believe I am marrying the same man, again. Suddenly, I realize why I can't believe it. It's because it isn't true. The man I am marrying tonight is not the same man. By the grace of Almighty God, Ronnie is a new creature in Christ Jesus. Hallelujah!

People gathered from near and far. Friends and relatives came from all across the country. I was very excited, filled with joy and profoundly grateful to God for giving us this opportunity to be so happy.

Little Jacqui, my adorable namesake, was our flower girl. Azlan was the ring bearer. Both of them were three years old at the time and just as cute as they could be. Jacqui stopped half way down the aisle so everyone could admire her.

When Azlan got to the front of the church, he threw the ring-pillow up in the air. Both of them thought that was so funny. We were glad we didn't put the rings on it. They came down the aisle to the tune of "Amazing Grace."

Ronnie and the groomsmen came down to the tune of "Praise the Lord My Brother," a very up beat gospel song that is shouting the victory. My best friend, Debbie Campbell, was my Matron of Honor. Our colors were black and white. There were over three hundred people in attendance. God is so good.

Needless to say, Ronnie's jaw dropped when I walked down the aisle, and his grin lit up the room. Everything went smoothly. I cried most of the night. Before Ronnie and I exchanged our vows, I read a poem I had written for him that morning. It reads as follows:

DEAR RONNIE

Dear Ronnie I've prayed and asked the Lord to give me the words to say,

To express to you my heart felt joy and love for you today.

I am so Blessed and thankful for all that God has done,
to get us in position, so that He could make us one.

I stand and look into your eyes and see a brand new man,
and have no fear, nor hesitate to give to you my hand.

Because God has convinced me, that He has made you whole,
and has prepared you as my mate, spirit, body and soul.

I commit to you my faithfulness to reverence and esteem,
you as my husband, from this day forth, we are a God made team.

I am elated that you chose me out from all the rest,

But God had promised both of us we'd have His very best.

So I stand before these witnesses, and say this night to you,

I give to you my all and all, my very best I'll do.

I had planned to just serve mints, peanuts and maybe some little open-faced sandwiches at the reception. But when Ronnie told Dennis that, he said, "No homeboy, we've got to do better than that." He bought some meat, cheese and relish trays. We also had punch.

We bought the wedding cake from the grocery store for one hundred and eighty dollars. We had that money, but things were getting tight. I must run on to tell you that they were very late delivering the cake. Some of the guests had left before the cake was delivered. Ronnie was upset about that. He asked, "Why are you so late? What happened?"

The guy said, "Well, to tell you the truth sir, we couldn't find the cake."

"Couldn't find it?"

"No sir, we looked and looked for it."

"Where were you looking for it?" Ronnie asked.

"In the freezer, where it was supposed to be," he replied.

"Where did you find it?"

"In the freezer," said the young man.

"What?"

"Yes, in the same freezer where we were looking but we couldn't see it and we don't know why. So because we are so late we want you to have the cake free and here are some grocery certificates for fifty dollars that you can redeem at any of our stores. We are so sorry for the mix up and the delay."

Now, do you want my take on the situation? I believe, with all my heart, that the Lord had an angel to stand in front of that cake until it was so late they felt they had to give it to us free. God's favor is better than money.

Rhonda worked for the Marriott hotel at that time. When she asked for time off to attend our wedding, her boss wanted to know the details. When she told him the whole story, he thought it was so great that we had reconciled. She told him we were going to San Diego on our honeymoon for a week. This man, whom we had never met, arranged for us to have a room at the Marriott in San Diego that overlooks the bay. To top it off, it had a view of Coronado Island. This room normally sells for two hundred and fifty dollars per night, but he gave it to us for thirty-nine dollars per night.

The wedding, reception and honeymoon were absolutely God. We had the time of our lives. Our friends showered us with gifts and money. We found out that God knows how to put on a wedding.

HEAVEN ON EARTH

Our wedding night was the greatest miracle of all. Before Ronnie and I had divorced, he could not maintain an erection with me. I believe it was partly because of all his infidelity. That was one of the reasons I didn't want him back.

That night at the hotel, at the instruction of our counselor, we prayed in the spirit before we made love. I'm tellin' you…it was the best Ronnie has ever made love to me in our lives. I thought, for a moment, he was twenty-one years old again. We looked each other in the eyes. He kept saying, with tears in his eyes, "Thank You, Jesus. Hallelujah. Praise You, Father. Thank You, Lord." It was Heaven on earth. We both cried tears of joy.

I will not go into any more detail. I don't want this book to get X-rated. Suffice to say that God, our Father, did a **supernatural** healing in his body; and, it continues until this day. The next morning, we flew off to San Diego for a week of more of the same.

CHAPTER 17

MARRIAGE GOD'S WAY

e came back from the most wonderful honeymoon any couple could ever have experienced. We settled into Ronnie's one-bedroom apartment. We had seen God put on a wedding. Now, we were ready to watch God show us how He intended marriage to be.

The first thing He told me was, "Shut up. Just stop talking so much. Do more listening to Ronnie and Me." I began to pray, *"Set a watch, O LORD, before my mouth; keep the door of my lips,* (Psalm 141:3). I'll *"let no corrupt communication proceed out of [my] mouth, but that which is good to the use of edifying, that it may minister grace unto the hearers,"* (Ephesians 4:29). Although it was difficult, I did pretty well.

Then the Lord told me, "If you ever become angry with Ronnie and want to argue, just come aside with Me before you do. Get alone. Ask Ronnie's permission to fast and we will work things out, together."

To come aside means fasting and praying, even if it is just for one day. I have faithfully done that. I've missed many meals; but, Ronnie and I don't argue. I didn't say we don't disagree on some things; but, we don't argue. When I do come aside, God always shows me *me*. I always have opportunity to pray and walk in love.

Ronnie has been consistent in prayer and getting his instructions from the Father. That's the first thing I saw was different in this marriage. His faith has grown stronger and stronger. He has taken his rightful place as the spiritual head of the family. I am still in awe of what God has done. But to be honest, at first, I was still waiting for the other shoe to drop. I know now that there is no other shoe.

LOVING EVERY MINUTE OF IT

The other thing I observed is that he has never stopped courting me. He has continued to romance me, until this day. He whispers in my ear and holds my hand. Ronnie calls me, breathing heavily on the phone, "This is an obscene phone call. Is this the cutie pie I made love to last night?" He is so funny and so much fun. I love every minute of my life.

He calls me almost everyday from work to say, "I love you and can't wait to get to you tonight." It's so great. We slow dance in front of the family room fireplace. We lie in bed, holding each other close and crying because we are so thankful for the mercy and grace God has shown to us. He gave us another chance to love one another. I know the world says that after the honeymoon is over you settle down to reality. Well, in a marriage that God designs, a honeymoon for life is reality.

We pray together and apart every day. We study the Word and talk about what the Lord is saying to us. We often find that He is telling us the same things, in different ways.

I never dreamed I could love anybody so deeply. This love is different from what we **thought** was love in the old marriage. As much as I tried to get Ronnie to change before, I could never have fixed him as well as God did when He recreated him. Truly, he is a new creature in Christ. Old things are passed away. There is not a trace of the old Ronnie left.

I've said that before and I will probably say it again. It **still** astounds me.

In our marriage, God's kingdom has come on earth as it is in Heaven. Many people still don't believe our marriage is as good as it really is. We have, from time to time, hesitated to tell them how much fun we're having. We had never been on a cruise before. Now, Ronnie takes me at least twice a year. That has become our favorite way to vacation.

REPAIRER OF THE BREACH

A few months after we were married, the Lord told us, "Go and tell what I have done in your lives. Tell the world and the church that I am in the marriage restoration business. Show people that My heart is reconciliation. Allow your marriage to be undeniable proof of Christ's love for the church. Be carriers of hope to an unbelieving, discouraged and hopeless world. Show them that I Am able to do anything, if they will allow Me to."

I said, "Lord, are You talking about a ministry?" It came to us so clearly. What is ministry if it isn't a demonstration of God's manifested power to do the impossible. What He has done in our lives was impossible for man. But it was possible for Him. He showed us that our marriage is His ministry to the world and the church. He kept saying "the church" because that's where the imposters spend their time. We know there are imposter pastors, whose marriages are a wreck. But, they won't seek help. They don't realize they sow those seeds of a bad marriage into their congregations. God is not pleased with that.

As we fasted and prayed, God woke us up one night, *"You shall be called the Repairer of the Breach."* We had read that scripture in Isaiah 58:12 many times as we fasted and prayed. His Words made so much sense to us–The Repairer of the Breach Ministries, Inc. Wow, He had this planned before the foundation of the earth.

People began asking us how we got back together. We would tell them it was God, our Father. He gave us instructions then gave us the grace to follow those instructions. Some people thought it was great and some thought it was phony. We didn't really care what they thought. We knew it was real and kept doing what God told us to do.

TELL THE TRUTH AND EXPOSE THE DEVIL

One day, I was curling my hair when the Lord said to me, "You're going on the radio." I thought maybe He wanted me to disc jockey again. Back in the seventies, I disc jockeyed, on radio, for years. Media is my background.

A few weeks later, I was turning the dial on my radio. I tuned into this new Christian station. I thought, "This must be it. I'll go down and apply for board operator." I did. When I came off the elevator, the station manager was coming out. He introduced himself and asked me to come to his office.

He told me that he didn't have any paid positions right then. But, he wanted to know where I was working now. I proceeded to tell him our story. He said, "You should have your own, weekly, radio broadcast to tell people this wonderful testimony."

"We don't have the money to do that."

"If I make it so you can afford it, will you?

"Yes." He worked a God kind of deal for us and The Repairer of the Breach Ministries went on the air. December 2005 will mark our ninth year on KLDC radio. We now do ministry on the internet. God opened a door for us to allow Him to repair breaches in marriages. The one thing we were impressed to do on the radio was to be real. God didn't call us to preach sermons. He called us to talk, seriously, to people about lying, cheating, adultery and drugs. Tell the truth and expose the devil. We are doing just that.

I tell people about the depression, alcohol and drugs that had me bound. While I am on this subject, alcohol is a drug. It is the legal, socially accepted drug in our culture that is killing millions, daily. But, that's another book. Ronnie talks, in detail, about the adultery, drugs, lies and everything that almost destroyed him. At first, I was shocked at some of the things he does share on the air.

This is how Ronnie opened the broadcast: "Hi, I'm Ronnie Calloway. Adultery took me farther than I wanted to go, kept me longer than I wanted to stay, and cost me more than I wanted to pay. But God has reconciled us, after seven years of separation and divorce."

Because we are completely healed and have forgiven one another, we have no more skeletons in the closet. To be more accurate, we even got rid of the closet. We are free, indeed, to love one another. We help other people who might be now where we once were.

We have seen marriages healed. Separated couples have come back together. Why? They have chosen to be obedient to the Word and will of God. Not everyone is willing to do whatever it takes to make their marriage work. Nonetheless, we minister to those who **are** willing; and, we point them to the Father.

Jesus Christ is always willing to heal, deliver, and take us to higher heights and deeper depths, in Him. When folks hear us talking about everything we went through, they locate themselves in our message; and, they hear hope.

Married men call my husband because they are having an affair and want to know how to get out. We don't let them call it an affair. We tell them it is adultery. It is sin. *The wages of sin is death* if you don't repent and come out of it. It can be the death of the relationship or it can be a physical death–depending on what you contract.

You would be surprised how many want to come out but just don't know how. I am so proud of Ronnie. He pulls no punches with them. He tells them in counseling, "What you just said to me is not true. I told those same lies for ten years. So, I recognize them when I hear them. It is only the truth that will make you free."

RESTORATION

As we have continued to be obedient to the Lord, He continues to bless us in every area of our lives. About a year after we were married, Ronnie said, "Jack, I believe if we go and look for a house God will give us one." I agreed.

God supernaturally gave us a three bedroom, brick house. Somehow, Ronnie's credit report was good. We don't know how; he was homeless for nine months, lost everything he had–including a house–and came out with good credit? We did *not* try to find out how. Again, God did a miracle.

In four years, that house appreciated so rapidly that we had approximately seventy thousand dollars in equity. We needed more room; so, we took some of the equity from that house and put it down on a larger, new home. The new home had almost as much equity in it as the other. The first house became our rental investment property.

Our new home also came with all new appliances, including a washer and dryer. Truly *God has restored the years that the locust have eaten, the cankerworm, the palmerworm and the caterpillar* (Joel 2:25). That scripture means more than that to me. God has restored us to a marriage the way He intended it to be in the Garden of Eden. We are eating the fruit of the tree of life.

A few years ago, Ronnie flew me to San Francisco for lunch. Ironically, we found ourselves at the same restaurant where I cried because I missed him so much. I shared that story with him. He embraced me, "Baby, you never have to cry again." I thought, as I cried tears of joy in his arms, does God cover every minute detail or what?

Ronnie is at the top of the pay scale on his job. We do biblical counseling, on a daily basis. We conduct seminars for married couples and singles at local churches. We are the marriage pastors at our church. On July 2, 2003, we were ordained and licensed by our Bishop, Rayfield Whittington, of the Word Up Life Changes Church. We are now able to marry couples ourselves–after they go through our counseling program for one year. *This is the lord's doings and it is marvelous in our eyes.* (Psalm 118:23*)*

THAT LOVE

I am so thankful to God for not letting me go. We will be married for 10 years on April 19, 2006. I've never been happier in my entire life. I am so glad that Jesus continued to love me, in spite of myself.

This is that love that would not let me go. When I screamed at God, He would not let me go. When I told Him how angry I was at Him, He would not let me go. When I turned my back on Him to sin, He would not let me go. No matter what I did, His Love would not let me go. Please read Romans 8 when you finish this book.

Ronnie's love would not let me go, either. After all we had gone through, he prayed and asked God to send me back to him. His love would not let me go. After all the questions and the third degree, he would not let me go. After me telling him, over and over again, he was not in my future, he would not let me go. In reality, it was God's love for me **through** him that would not let me go.

How I shudder to think where I would be today if they had let me go. I know that I would have gone the way of the world. We always do when God is not directing our paths. We, as humans, have a tendency to get off the paths God has planned for us. We go down the alleys of life. Those alleys are where hidden traps lie in wait for our wandering feet and minds.

Mama used to tell me, "If you don't know where you're going, you'll wind up somewhere else." How can we possibly know where we are going if God is not leading us there? (See Proverbs 20:24) Just think, I would have missed my purpose. I would have missed Ronnie and I enjoying the love and admiration of our children and grandchildren together. We would have missed taking our grandchildren on a cruise to the Caribbean together and seeing their smiling faces–faces which look just like ours.

RECONCILIATION

I would have missed the very reason for which I was born. That reason is to give God pleasure, while being an example of His love and forgiveness to the world. I would have missed the honor of writing this phenomenal love story. I would have missed this opportunity to share how strong the love of God is for **you**.

Oh, how much He loves you and wants to fulfill your every need and heart's desire. You would not have this particular example of how willing God is to use His ability in **your** behalf. I would not have had this platform to encourage you to write your own personal love story. Had I continued to say no to God, I would have missed it all. Don't you say no to Him.

I went through all that I did so I could stand, flat-footed, in complete confidence and say, "God loves you with an everlasting love. Beneath you are His everlasting arms. There is nothing too hard for Him. Never, ever settle for less than the very best God has for you. Moreover, only He can show you who, what and where that is; and, only He can gently lead you there."

No matter what your situation may be, God wants to reconcile it, heal it, recreate it or restore it—better than it has ever been. Please allow Him to do so. He is in relentless pursuit of you. His **love will not let you go.**

Thank You, Father, for **Your** Love that would not let **me** go!

EPILOGUE

Lord, You have blessed me with a love in my marriage that is far, far greater than any love I've ever known. You have given me a husband who loves You, first and foremost. He is a God fearing man, who has allowed You to teach him how to love me, supernaturally.

Father, I feel so fortunate that You have chosen me to be the recipient of this God-kind of love–love that will not let me go. Lord, when I see, day by day, how tender and kind Ronnie is to me, I can hardly contain my gratefulness to You and him. I realize, Lord, that You are the source of the deep love and affection we share with one another. I can hardly write this for crying great, big tears of joy.

Thank You, Father, for snatching me out of the grips of Satan–when I willfully rebelled against Your will and went after my own pleasure. Thank You, for making a way of escape for me back to You and Your arms of safety. I love You, Lord, and will be forever grateful.

But, Lord, I still wonder, Why me? There are so many women, who love and are obedient to You, from beginning to end. They don't get to live the awesome life You have given me with Ronnie. Why me? I know it is not because of anything special I have done Lord, so why me? Lord, is it because of Mama's prayers? Is it because she had to spend some extra time on her knees for me? Or, is it because she gave me back to You, when I was born? I don't know why, Lord, but, I thank You.

This marriage and our love for each other is truly an example of Christ's love for the church. I just wish that everyone could know this kind of love in marriage. Lord, thank You for Ronnie. I could never have thought to ask for a more loving, kind, sweet, gentle, strong, peaceful, take charge, rich man of God—not in a million years. He is much more than I could have ever asked or thought. Thank You. Thank You. Thank You.

—Jackie

Ronnie & Jackie Calloway

ABOUT THE AUTHOR

acqueline Calloway's journey began in Huntington, West Virginia. She was the eighth of nine children, born to Willie and Lillie M. Smith.

Shortly after graduating from Huntington High School, she moved to Colorado and began a career in television broadcasting. During her career, she worked as a community news reporter for KOA radio and later for the CBS affiliate station in Denver. Most notably, while at PBS affiliate KRMA, she became the executive producer and host of the groundbreaking, weekly television show *Aisha*. She had the distinction of being one of the first, black, female television hosts. As such, she helped pave the way for other African-American broadcasters to follow.

In 1986, Jackie became an Associate Council Director for the Rocky Mountain Conference of the United Methodist Church Headquarters.

Over the next 10 years, Jackie developed programs in cultural aware-
ness and spiritual development for two hundred and forty-four
churches in Colorado, Wyoming, and Utah.

In 1997, Jackie and her husband Ronnie, became marriage coun-
selors and launched The Repairer of the Breach Ministries on radio
KLDC. The program has successfully run for over eight years. Ronnie
and Jackie Calloway are ordained ministers. In the not-too-distant
future, they will expand their ministry to the world-wide-web,
repairing breaches in marriages and relationships around the world.

Ronnie and Jackie reside in Denver and have three daughters and
five of the most beautiful, intelligent grandchildren in the world.

Jackie Calloway
P.O. Box 473368
Aurora, Colorado 80047
303-832-1811
repairer@earthlink.net
repairerofthebreachministries.org